FLOWER PETALS FALL,
BUT THE FLOWER ENDURES

JAPAN LIBRARY

FLOWER PETALS FALL, BUT THE FLOWER ENDURES

The Japanese Philosophy of Transience

TAKEUCHI SEIICHI

Japan Publishing Industry Foundation for Culture

Japanese names are given in Japanese order,
with surname preceding personal name.

Flower Petals Fall, but the Flower Endures:
The Japanese Philosophy of Transience
Takeuchi Seiichi
Translated and published by
Japan Publishing Industry Foundation for Culture (JPIC)
3-12-3 Kanda-Jinbocho, Chiyoda-ku, Tokyo 101-0051, Japan

First paperback edition: January 2019

© 2011 Takeuchi Seiichi
English translation © 2019
Japan Publishing Industry Foundation for Culture
All rights reserved

Originally produced by KADOKAWA GAKUGEI SHUPPAN and
published in Japanese under the title *Hanabira wa chiru hana wa chiranai:
Mujō no nihon shisō*, by KADOKAWA CORPORATION, Tokyo.
English publishing rights arranged with KADOKAWA CORPORATION.
This paperback English edition is a revised and edited version of the
original hardcover English edition by JPIC in 2015.

Book design by Miki Kazuhiko, Ampersand Works

Printed in Japan
ISBN 978-4-86658-069-2
http://www.jpic.or.jp/japanlibrary/

CONTENTS

Note to the Reader about Romanization viii

PREFACE ix

CHAPTER
1
Mujōkan in Contemporary Japan
The Sublimity (*Shōgon*) of "Emptiness Is Form" (*Kūsokuzeshiki*) 1

Mujōkan in Contemporary Japan 2
What Is the Meaning of *Hakanai*? 5
Proposals Made by Karaki Junzō 7
Methodology 8
The Argument of "Man's Peace of Mind" 10
Recognition of *Onozukara* 13
A View of Life and Death Where "We Become *Mu* When We Die" 15
Recognition of *Mizukara* 17
To Do *Mizukara* and to Become *Onozukara* 20
Mizukara = *Onozukara* 22
Mizukara ≠ *Onozukara* 23
Mizukara = ≠ *Onozukara* 25
"Man Is Still Sublime" 27
The *Shōgon* of *Mizukara* and *Onozukara* 31

CHAPTER
2
What Is the Meaning of *Tōtoi?* 37

On Reason 38
On Mystery (with Particular Reference to Life) 40
On Activeness 47
Ichigū-ness 50
Once-ness: Being a One and Only 52
Unusualness (Gratitude) 1 (Fate) 54
Unusualness (Gratitude) 2 (Time) 58
Shikisokuzekū Kūsokuzeshiki 63
Relationality (the Soul [*Tamashii*]) 64
Itamu, Tomurau 69

CHAPTER
3
Re-Visiting "Flower Petals Fall, but the Flower Endures" 73

The Direction of *Tomurai* and *Itami* in Miyazawa Kenji 74
From "Beloved Ones" to "Everyone's Happiness" 78
A Single Spirit and the Pure Love for Everyone 81
From the Living to the Dead, and From the Dead to the Living 85
How to Render *Itoshisa* 91

CHAPTER
4
What Is *Shiawase?* 95

Shiawase 96
Medetashi 99

Iwau 102
Omoshiroshi 104
Sakiwau and *Saiwai* 111
Musubi 113
Life and Death 117
Mujō and *Onozukara* 121
The Many Meanings of *Sumu* 125

CHAPTER
5
The *Awai* between *Onozukara* and *Mizukara* 131

Theoretical Framework of the *Awai* between *Onozukara* and *Mizukara* 132
Awai as an Issue in Japanese Philosophy 133
Awai as a Standpoint from which to View Contemporary Philosophy 134
The *Awai* in *Fullmetal Alchemist* 137
The Meanings of *Onozukara* and *Mizukara* 141
The Ambiguity of *Onozukara* 144
Onozukara as Otherness 148
Sakaguchi Ango's View of *Onozukara* 150
Omnipresent *Onozukara* and Partial *Mizukara* 154
Solidification of *Mizukara* and the Problem of the "I" 158
Awai 162
Further Discussion of "It Turns Out that We Will Get Married" 164
The Ethics of the *Awai* 166
Yasashi 169
Kanashi 175
Sayōnara 179

BIBLIOGRAPHY 183
INDEX 189

NOTE TO THE READER ABOUT ROMANIZATION

This book employs the modified Hepburn system in which *n* rather than *m* is used before syllables beginning with *m*, *b*, or *p*; an apostrophe follows *n* when *n* is part of the preceding syllable and the following syllable begins with *yo*, *yu*, or a vowel; macrons indicate long vowels. Romanization of classical Japanese follows modern orthography (*gendai kanazukai*) rather than historical orthography (*rekishiteki kanazukai*).

Japanese names are given in Japanese order, with surname preceding personal name. The titles of Japanese books are given in romanization followed by an English translation in parentheses on first appearance, and thereafter in English only. Exceptions are given to the appearance of the *Kojiki* and the *Man'yōshū* which include the English translation in parentheses on first appearance, and thereafter in Japanese only. Publication details can be found in the Bibliography.

PREFACE

This is a study of the Japanese concept of *mujō*—the transience of life. It was inspired by the words of Kaneko Daiei, a modern Japanese Buddhist philosopher: "Flower petals fall, but the flower endures. The form perishes, but the being endures."

"The enduring flower" may be thought of as the "soul" (*tamashii*), though it should not necessarily be considered a substantial entity. By way of illustration, it can be seen as akin to the depiction of the soul in the short story *Jojōka* (A Lyrical Poem) by Kawabata Yasunari (1899–1972), in which he states that "the word 'soul' is nothing but a modifier of the power that permeates the whole of creation."

The protagonist of *A Lyrical Poem* tries to reconcile his irrepressible yearnings for his dead lover by placing them in the grand flow of the whole of creation. He expresses his feelings in poetic terms, as in "I find myself and you in the fauna and flora" and "You and I will become flowers of the rose, plum, and oleander, to which butterflies carry pollen to join us in marriage."

This imaginative fantasy is "the culmination of a sadness of the human tendency toward attachment" which arose, the protagonist states, because "I loved you too much." As I explain in this book, this understanding of the "soul" overlaps with the depictions of the personae in the Noh drama of Zeami (ca. 1363–1443) and is further linked to the thinking of Shiga Naoya (1883–1971) that, though the one and only "self" lives and dies, still "I am a water drop in a mighty river, which is sufficient." "Tamashii no yukue" (Where Souls Go), by the folklorist Yanagita Kunio (1875–1962), is also relevant in this context.

This thinking applies both to the flower petals that fall and to the flower that endures. In short, hereafter I will try to shed some light on this subject by discussing the key terms *onozukara* (spontaneity) and *mizukara* (voluntariness). When the voluntary (*mizukara*) actions of human beings are displaced by grand spontaneous (*onozukara*) functions, the values, meanings, "playfulness," and sublimity (*shōgon*) of *mizukara* appear at the boundaries (*awai*) between them. These concepts form the underpinnings of Japanese *mujō* philosophy, which I hope will become clearer in the text that follows.

Takeuchi Seiichi

CHAPTER 1

Mujōkan in Contemporary Japan

The Sublimity (*Shōgon*) of "Emptiness Is Form" (*Kūsokuzeshiki*)

We should no longer look for a means of
escape. We have no choice but to carry
the *mujō*-ness of *mujō* to its ultimate end.

Karaki Junzō

Mujōkan in Contemporary Japan

What I would like to take up first is the situation in modern Japan concerning *mujōkan* and nihilism. *Mujōkan* is the Buddhist concept of the impermanence of worldly things. *Mujō* means "impermanent"; *kan* means "view."

It is ironic that Japanese children today, who you would expect to be full of life and potential, should have to be instilled with a "zest for living," which is a notion being promoted under governmental curriculum guidelines. This lack of a zest for living is not, of course, limited to minors, but is also true of adults, who are worn down by the environment around them. The number of midlife suicides is increasing, indicating a feeling of *hakanasa* (fleetingness) or *munashisa* (emptiness) that is pervasive throughout society.

I will not easily forget the personal impact of some statistics announced at a symposium held quite some time ago; they were from a questionnaire conducted by the Child Research Institute for a project led by the writer Kurokawa Sō and others, and constitute, in a sense, the basis of what occupies my mind these days. When elementary-school fifth and sixth graders and junior high school students were asked if humanity would become extinct in their lifetime, more than half of the elementary school students and almost sixty percent of the junior high school students (particularly boys) answered in the affirmative. (Takeuchi Seiichi, ed., *Mukonkyo no jidai* [A Time without Foundation])

This kind of questionnaire can, of course, be interpreted in many ways. Interestingly, it also contained the question "What will the 21st century be like?" to which many of the children gave rose-tinted, sci-fi-like responses. While it is true that we should take such figures with a grain of salt, the fact that more than half of the children thought that mankind might disappear during their lifetime struck me as quite extraordinary.

The philosopher of religion Inoue Nobutaka, who was in attendance at the symposium, had conducted a survey of 4,000 university students concerning religion. He reported that when asked whether they believed in such end-of-the-world predictions as the prophecies of Nostradamus, more than forty percent replied that they "believed" or "somewhat believed" them.

Indeed, young people nowadays possess a rich vocabulary and awareness concerning the end of the world. We cannot help but note that the literature and anime they are most familiar with assume that the world will come to an end.

This is a *fin de siècle* sentiment, and even though we have entered a new century, the feeling that the world (mankind) might soon end still looms over us; in fact, the political and social situation after the 9/11 terrorist attacks has given it added momentum. Thus, it should come as no surprise that traditionally accepted meanings and motivations—such as the will to form an orderly society—have been eroded and are beginning to crumble. The individual has become unable to establish a rationale for existence from the viewpoint of the society in which he or she exists. Nihilism in this sense has become pervasive.

Although there are various approaches to how we should grasp this situation, and while we shouldn't unnecessarily foment a sense of crisis, it is still important, I believe, to give some thought to the pervasive feeling that life is purposeless and fleeting.

In the West, of course, nihilism began to be thematically explored by Nietzsche in the late 19th century, but about the same time there was a spiritual crisis or *hanmon jōkyō* in which Japanese intellectuals found themselves unable to give a credible reason for mankind's existence and the world we live in.

The situation was so grave that the inability to answer this question sometimes had fatal consequences. Fujimura Misao (1886–1903), a philosophy student who committed suicide at the age of seventeen, wrote the following in a farewell poem: "Indeed, [the world is] incomprehensible. I have decided to end my life with this anguished thought." However, this gravity was somewhat tempered by the idea that, as the novelist Dazai Osamu (1909–48) said, "Downfall doesn't occur during the darkest hours." While this anguish manifested itself in gloomy, nihilistic ways, it also had sundry nuances and was expressed with considerable feeling.

What is the present situation?

While it is true that hard questions and a sense of crisis still remain, it is almost as if they have lost their color in a brilliant, overexposed landscape. They look strangely bright, and people seem to question things without much seriousness, or perhaps not question them at all. Against this overexposed background, people (especially young people) seem to be saddled with an undefined sense of fatigue.

"What came out of nothingness returned to nothingness—that's all," murmured the protagonist of the novel *1973 nen no pinbōru* (Pinball, 1973), an early work by Murakami Haruki, a contemporary bestselling writer. This sentiment is undoubtedly shared by present-day young people, together with the main characters in Murakami's later works.

This is, without a doubt, an example of *mujōkan*, or nihilism. In the following section we will break down this general situation into specific topics and consider whether it is possible to give them a more positive interpretation.

What Is the Meaning of *Hakanai*?

Hakanai is a very common word that is, nonetheless, crucial to our discussion. Its literal meaning is *haka ga* (is) *nai* (not)—i.e., there is no *haka*. *Haka* originally referred to the extent or amount of rice or other crop that was planted or expected to be harvested. It appears in the phrases *haka ga iku* and *hakadoru* (make good progress). That is, the fundamental meaning of *hakanai* is that results cannot be guaranteed despite one's best efforts, or the desired outcome is not to be had, from which the secondary meanings are derived: lacking in substance, unresponsive, or disappointing. (*Iwanami kogo jiten* [Iwanami Classical Japanese Dictionary])

Hakanai is also equal to *hakaru koto ga dekinai* (be unable to hakaru). *Hakaru* is the verbalized form of *haka*, and so *hakanai* signifies a negative condition in which it is impossible to *hakaru*.

The various meanings of *hakaru* are easier to classify when seen in *kanji*. For example, 計る, 量る, and 測る mean to measure. 衡る and 忖る mean to coordinate, arrange, or assume based on such measurement. 諮る in 会議に諮る (*kaigi ni hakaru*) means to present a topic for discussion at a conference. Further, we have 図る, 策る, and 謀る, which mean to propose or plan something based on such coordination, arrangement, or conjecture.

In short, *hakaru* is a fundamental practice necessarily required when people live with a certain purpose or plan in mind. This is particularly true in modern times when scientific and technological ideas have received special emphasis. The basic notion of science and technology is a numerical measurement with *hakari* (scales), on the basis of which plans for the future are developed.

This is especially prevalent in so-called business (busy-ness) societies, which demand that *haka* be promptly realized and the desired results be accomplished. Western "*pro*active" attitudes or "*pro*spective" time consciousness is manifested in such words as "project," "produce," "promotion," and "progress," notions which the modern West intrinsically embraces. (Washida Kiyokazu, *Oi no kūhaku* [The Vacuity of Old Age])

However, the very foundation of *haka* is now being undermined. We can no longer successfully *hakaru* (measure, arrange, or plan) the world or society in which we live since we are at a point where people feel the imminent extinction of mankind or the end of the world. They have begun to feel ineffective and to proactively seek other meanings and purposes behind hitherto accepted concepts. It is in this context that a condition of *hakanai* has emerged.

Although the word *hakanai* has obvious negative connotations, it also has something positive—something that is only possible under the conditions described as *hakanai*. In other words, *hakanai* is not just a sentiment. Being properly conscious of it, we can retrieve what we have lost in the busyness of a primarily business-oriented society. Significantly, the components forming the *kanji* for "busy" (忙) literally mean "mind killing."

That is, instead of digitizing everything and seeking results further and further into the future, we should repossess the pricelessness of "being here and now," not subject to the jurisdictions of *hakaru*.

Proposals Made by Karaki Junzō

As early as 1963 the critic and philosopher Karaki Junzō (1904–80) declared:

> There is hardly any other period in history that unashamedly displays the effects of *mujō* as today. The conditions we live in are *mujō* itself. Dare I say it: nihilism has become so prevalent and universalized that it can no longer be distinctively perceived. Nihilism no longer refers to a certain doctrine or to the thought of a certain person. The whole world is nihilistic…
>
> As we prosper and progress, so we become ever more insecure. That this prosperity and progress

might lead to death and extinction is the fear that
dominates the reality of the world.

(*Mujō* [Impermanence])

The above extract was written more than forty years ago, but its perception of the times is no worse for the wear; rather, it now signifies the global reality more than ever. Karaki, based on this perception, further declared:

We should no longer look for a means of escape. We have no choice but to carry the *mujō*-ness of *mujō* to its ultimate end. (*Impermanence*)

Mujō here is synonymous with nihilism. But certain questions arise: what does it mean to carry the *mujō*-ness (nihilism) of *mujō* (the nihil) to its ultimate end, what new avenues open up by doing so, and does it go no further than deepening the fleetingness of *hakanai*? Of course, although Karaki's nihilism is supposed to transmute into something positive in its thoroughness, its ideological content can still be called into question.

Methodology

These issues will continue to be the object of our consideration hereafter. However, what Karaki did specifically in his book was to make a painstaking genealogical investigation into how such words as *hakanashi* (a literary form of *hakanai*) and *mujō* were once employed; his goal was to reconsider clichéd expressions whose specific meanings have been lost, such as *shogyō mujō* (everything is transient) or *issai kaikū* (all is empty). For Karaki, this act was not meant as a search for "a means of escape."

When it comes to how people live, it is quite obvious that new lifestyles cannot be created independently of what has come before. The question becomes: how can we speak of older things in a living language suited to the modern age?

As the philosophical and intellectual environment of *hakanai* is brought into question under conditions reflecting modern times, a consideration of the conditions themselves is obviously indispensable, though, needless to say, clever manipulation must clearly be avoided. The more advanced and fundamental the conditions are, the more they must be examined by drawing from the stock of questions that have been posed heretofore.

In the chaos of the postwar period Yanagita Kunio experienced a sense of crisis about what the *ie* (the Japanese household) would be in the future. He remarked:

> What will households be like, or what should they be like? What do people wish them to be, at least in regard to our time? To answer these questions it is necessary to know some basic facts. Unfortunately, however, public officials since the Meiji period have found such preliminary work to be too troublesome and have tried to ignore this important issue.
>
> (*Senzo no hanashi* [About Our Ancestors])

One can sense the depth of Yanagita's seriousness when he

quietly says, "To answer these questions it is necessary to know some basic facts." He suggests that the contemporary crisis arises from the fact that we cannot discuss the shoulds and should nots of what our *ie* should be in the future without the preliminary work of learning how the *ie* has existed to present; yet, since the Meiji period, we have failed to do this important work. Yanagita's massive academic efforts were in effect that preliminary work.

This vividly brings to mind a remark that the Japanese shogi master Habu Yoshiharu (b. 1970) once made in an interview. He said that what occupies his mind during a long game is not the different possible responses of his opponent to his next move, though he naturally thinks about that too, but more often he is reviewing the process from the first move to the present situation. That is, in reviewing how the present situation emerged, his next move spontaneously arises. I felt that this made perfect sense.

Now I would like, after the fashion of Karaki, to place the ideological issues mentioned above in the stream of thought from modern times to the present day for the purpose of reexamination.

The Argument of "Man's Peace of Mind"

Fukuzawa Yukichi (1835–1901), who brought Enlightenment to modern Japan, wrote an essay in his later years entitled "Ningen no anshin" (Man's Peace of Mind) in the book *Fuku-ō hyakuwa* (One Hundred Discourses of Fukuzawa).

In this essay he states that the sun, moon and earth are mere specks when considered against the backdrop of the infinite universe, adding that:

> Man is no better than an unthinking, feeble creature much like a maggot. In a flash he happens to breathe, to sleep, and to eat in this world, driven by his emotions, and just as quickly, like a night's dream, he disappears, leaving no trace.

After putting forward this view of mankind, he takes it as a base and paradoxically deduces how man can achieve "peace of mind." Elsewhere he proposes the idea that peace of mind comes from the realization that from the beginning, there was nothing (*honrai muichibutsu*). By this he means that man enters the world with nothing and departs with nothing.

Fukuzawa once remarked that he was able to take a rather carefree approach to administering Keiō Gijuku (subsequently Keio University) and the newspaper *Jiji Shinpō*, both of which he founded, because they did not exist before he established them and he could discontinue their operation whenever he chose. In other words, if he thought that he must not, at any cost, close them down, his mind would be in a constant state of worry. However, if he thought that they didn't exist before he created them, he could terminate their operation at any moment, allowing him to conduct negotiations and make decisions rather lightly. He believed that people who thought in this way would be more active and successful in business.

Fukuzawa's equation of man with a maggot and his comparison of life to a lighthearted game may be rather surprising, especially coming from an educator of his stature. However, by expressing his views in this way, Fukuzawa arrived at a certain peace of mind and vitality. On this basis, he explains that mankind is to be revered as the lord of creation (*banbutsu no rei*) because he has the intellectual capacity to foresee the future. Fukuzawa thus reverses his previous logic and holds man in high esteem. This is the familiar image that Japanese have of Fukuzawa, the person who enlightened us about the nobility (*tōtosa*) of humanity. According to Karaki, this change in point of view would be an example of a positive way of living emerging by pushing transience to the extreme.

The journalist, political theorist, and statesman Nakae Chōmin (1847–1901), an advocate of people's rights, developed a similar argument in his philosophy known as Nakae-ism:

> The world never began nor ends; it is eternally abundant and infinite. It is a vast profusion. However, its essence consists of a small number of elements that permanently detach, combine, and dissolve, and then detach, combine, and dissolve again, never decreasing nor increasing one iota; they are neither arising nor ceasing. Everything—plants, animals, and man—is born by combination and dies by dissolution.
> (*Zoku ichinen yūhan* [Sequel to a Year and a Half])

Nakae's philosophy is a "simple physical theory" to reduce the essence of the world (including mankind) to a small number of elements. From this perspective, he denies the existence of gods and spirits, for he believes that they are the convenient imaginings of human beings, who are "terrified of death, burn with a love for life, and desirous of preserving their identity as unique individuals."

However, it was by means of adhering to this anti-humanistic physical theory that Nakae was able to vigorously promote the "people's rights" of liberty and equality in the Meiji period. Even after he was informed that he had only a year and a half more to live, he enjoyed the rest of his life in comfort. By focusing on the "anti-" (*mu*), of anti-religion and anti-spiritualism, he was able to acquire a positive view of life.

Recognition of *Onozukara*

Both Fukuzawa and Nakae are illustrative of Karaki's assertion that working through the negativities of *mujō* and nihilism leads paradoxically to a certain positive peace of mind, vitality, reverence for human life, and the concepts of liberty and equality. Obviously, this understanding of negativity or *mu* is not that of *Nichts* (nothingness) in a Western context. Rather, when subjected to thoroughgoing examination, it is seen to be a field or function of awareness; in other words, it is the discovery or confirmation of spontaneous *onozukara*.

Fukuzawa's essay "Man's Peace of Mind" is the seventh essay in his *One Hundred Discourses of Fukuzawa*. The essay is narrated in a context to reveal the *onozukara* functions of heaven and the universe, including the first essay "Uchū" (The Universe), the second "Tenkō" (The Work of Heaven), and the third "Tendō hito ni ka-nari" (Man Can Follow the Way of Heaven). In one passage directed at unraveling the workings of *onozukara* in the heavens and universe, he writes, "Everything continually moves and continually changes, lives accordingly and dies accordingly"; however, "the great mechanism of the universe and nature is so subtle and mysterious that everything on this earth, from man down to animals, plants, and specks of dust, evades comprehension."

The idea of equating man with a maggot and regarding life as a game would amount to mere nihilism if broached without this metaphysical framework. This spontaneous *onozukara* framework is the basic premise of Fukuzawa's ideas. He criticizes and dismisses religion as nothing more than "an addiction," and yet he remains convinced that the great mechanism of the universe and nature works spontaneously (*onozukara*) in a subtle and mysterious manner. This may be different from what Fukuzawa refers to as religion, but one could say that it has a boundless religious, metaphysical conviction to it.

This is also true of Nakae Chōmin. Nakae denies the existence of gods, buddhas and the soul based on his "simple physical theory," but he accepts everything as being within an eternal abundance or vast profusion, which never began nor ends and is infinite. The essence of the abundance is a few elements, combining and dissolving, but in total never decreasing nor increasing in the least; that is, they are neither arising nor ceasing. He thinks that we emerge from this great abundance and again vanish into it. From this Nakae developed his unique, liberal view of life and death and also his ideals of freedom and equality.

Here is another, more symbolic example of *onozukara* from Shiga Naoya's novel *An'ya kōro* (A Dark Night's Passing). The main character, careworn from personal issues, comes to gain a certain peace of mind near the end of the novel.

> Burned out though he was, he felt an enigmatic euphoria. He now felt both his body and spirit melting into this Vast Nature. This Nature was invisible, like an indefinitely vast vapor enveloping him, who was the size of a poppy seed. The feeling of melting into it, being reduced to it, gave him a pleasure that could not be put into words.

He discovered "a Vast Nature" in Daisen, the site of a volcano in Tottori prefecture, where he was currently staying, and gained peace of mind by dissolving and reducing himself into that Nature, as if he were a tiny poppy seed. This is a typical example of how the recognition of man as being reduced to almost nothing leads to the discovery of the *onozukara* of "the Vast Nature" that embraces the tiniest of the tiny.

A View of Life and Death Where "We Become *Mu* When We Die"

Intellectuals in modern Japan, including Fukuzawa, Nakae, and Shiga, often hold a view of life and death in which "we become *mu* (nullity) when we die." Seen in the light of our present context, however, *mu* is far from being nothing; rather it means that we go back again to the Vast Nature or the Great Universe from which we came. This is why a kind of peace of mind or solace can occur when one says, "We become *mu* when we die."

When we use the word *mujō*, we do so with the recognition that *mu* simultaneously refers to the changeability of life around us and to the transience of the spontaneous *onozukara* world of nature. This understanding dates back to premodern times. To cite just one example, the 8th-century *Man'yōshū* (Collection of Ten Thousand Leaves) includes the following poem by Ōtomo no Yakamochi entitled "Yononaka no mujō o kanashiburu uta" (Lament for the Transient World):

> From the far beginning of heaven and earth,
> People have long said from mouth to mouth
> That the world is transient;
> When we turn to look up at the heavens,
> The shining moon waxes and wanes;
> On the treetops in the mountains
> Flowers bloom when spring comes;
> With the advent of autumn, with dew and frost,
> The colored leaves fall when the wind gusts;
> This is the earthly life of man.
> Rosy cheeks fade,
> Black hair grizzles,
> Morning smiles are gone in the evening.
> Looking at how worldly things change,
> Invisible as the wind,
> Endless as flowing water,
> I cannot help but weep in the garden.

This is a lament for the *mujō* of the world. The latter part of the poem describes the different aspects of *mujō* in our physical beings and the world around us, as shown in the phrase "Rosy cheeks fade, Black hair grizzles," while the earlier part narrates the transitions of nature, including the waxing and waning of the moon and seasonal changes. Thus we can see that the poet has overlapped the *mujōkan* in the latter part with the transitions of nature.

In short, the *onozukara* functions of nature are perceived here as transient phases, such as the trials of living, aging, disease, and death, which are both galling and inexorable facts of human life, and also overlapped by the great functions of heaven and earth, or nature. These functions—which the Buddhist priest Shinran (1173–1263) saw as coinciding with those of Amida (Amitabha) Buddha and the scholar Motoori Norinaga (1730–1801) saw as overlapping with the *kami* (or gods)—will be discussed later.

Recognition of *Mizukara*

The previous section showed how the effort to understand *mujō*-ness leads to the discovery of the *onozukara* of the Vast Nature that lies behind it. On the other hand, there is another important matter, which is the flip side of the coin: the discovery of *onozukara* leads to a confirmation of *mizukara* (the self).

In the aforementioned example in Shiga Naoya's novel, the existence of the self is regarded as small as a poppy seed, which eventually dissolves into Vast Nature. However, to put it the other way around, this leads to a reevaluation of the self as a transitory thing.

This is stated more clearly in Shiga's well-known passage in his essay "Nairu no mizu no itteki" (A Drop in the Nile):

> It is beyond our imagination how many million years have passed since man came into being, and in that passage of time countless people were born, lived, and died. I was born as one of them and am now living, but I am as a drop of water in the grandly flowing Nile, the only drop that is me for all time; even if you go back scores of thousands of years, you cannot find another me, and even though scores of thousands of years pass, I will not be born again. Still, I am a drop in a mighty river, which is sufficient.

This passage has the same structure as the discussion above in that "I" is defined as a tiny entity within a greater whole, but based on this recognition, it redefines the existence of the tiny self. The self is indeed a drop of water, but it is confirmed as a drop that is found nowhere else, even should you go back scores of thousands of years in the past or scores of thousands of years in the future. That is, it is simultaneously recognized that the existence of my self is but a drop in a great river, and that this drop is but one among many and exists only once. The significance of the fact that these two recognitions are made at the same time will be revealed in the following.

To that end it is worth referring to the concept of *ichigū/hitosumi* ("a corner") as it appears in Saichō's (767–822) "lightening a corner" and Dōgen's (1200–53) "a corner as a special place." In modern times the religious philosopher Uchimura Kanzō (1861–1930) used the phrase "stand in a corner," and more recently the ethicist Sagara Tōru (1921–2000) has given attention to this concept. I will confine myself to introducing how Uchimura speaks on this topic.

> Man is too limited in ability to occupy or take possession of a place on the limitless bedrock of infinite wisdom. What he can do is to take up a position in a small *ichigū* (corner) of this rock. If he can only cling to this *ichigū*, he will immediately be able to settle down and feel at peace; this rock is that strong. This explains why there are so many different religious sects, each of which is successful.
>
> (*Yo wa ikanishite kirisuto shinto to narishika* [How I Became a Christian])

In short, he believes that the Absolute cannot be perceived in its entirety but only one particular corner that is linked to the larger whole. However, our understanding of the self (*mizukara*) holds that the existence of the self is only the existence of one corner, and yet since it is a corner of the larger whole for that very reason this corner, as a corner, is in a sense the Absolute itself. This is Uchimura's way of thinking about the *ichigū*.

The notion of *yaoyorozu no kamigami* ("the eight million gods") that is so essential in Japanese mythology does not merely mean that a myriad gods exist all over the place, but is the idea that all over the place there are different, relative ways of being but that they all express the Absolute. While these days you hear this and that kind of question about monotheistic faith, there is in this concept an important hint that Japanese religion is not merely a relativism based on "you do your thing and we do ours."

To Do *Mizukara* and to Become *Onozukara*

The simultaneous realization that we exist as a mere drop in a great river and as an absolute drop that has never occurred before and will never occur again leads, in the famous words of the novelist Natsume Sōseki (1867–1916), to the simultaneous recognition of *sokuten kyoshi* and *jiko hon'i*. *Sokuten kyoshi* means to leave the self and follow the spontaneous functions of Great Heaven (Nature or *onozukara*). *Jiko hon'i* means to live our *mizukara* lives to the full. They are seemingly contradictory, but the co-establishment of the two seems integral to Sōseki's literature.

To cite just one example from Sōseki's novel *Sorekara* (And Then), there is a scene in which the main character decides to win back an old girlfriend. This act of self-determination is described as "returning to the bygone days of Nature" and "following the Will of Heaven." This means that pursuit of *jiko hon'i* is made in the form of following the functions of Heaven and leaving the self (*sokuten kyoshi*). Here we can see the thinking that voluntary *mizukara* decisions and actions follow the spontaneous *onozukara* of Nature and Heaven. According to *Tetsugaku nyūmon* (An Introduction to Philosophy) by Miki Kiyoshi (1897–1945), this notion means that "our acts, while done by ourselves, are simply what happens to turn out." The issue of *onozukara* and *mizukara* form a basic framework that I have been contemplating for some time, have discussed before, and will repeatedly bring up in this book. The starting point for my interest in the issue was how we should approach the overlapping of doing (*mizukara*) and turning out (*onozukara*).

In written Japanese, *onozukara* and *mizukara* both contain the kanji 自 (self)—自ら for *mizukara* and 自ずから for *onozukara*. Behind this is the understanding that what was done voluntarily (*mizukara*), and what has turned out to be (*onozukara*), are not two separate things.

We often hear phrases such as "it turns out that we will get married" or "it turns out that I have found a job." These expressions show a perception that, though the person made a decision and carried it out *mizukara*, it also "turns out" by virtue of a certain *onozukara*.

The same state of things can be found in the word *dekiru* (can do). *Dekiru* originally meant *idekuru* or "emerge" or "turn up." It is thought that the word *idekuru* came to have the meaning of possibility because people believed things were brought into realization by the establishment or emergence of a certain result or outcome by virtue of not only proactive efforts and acts of *mizukara*, but also by the workings of *onozukara*. We can see the same idea in the auxiliary verbs *-raru* or *-rareru*, which indicate passivity as well as possibility.

The following interesting example appears in the book *Nihongo ga mieru to eigo mo mieru* (You Can Understand English If You Can Understand Japanese) by the critic and English literature scholar Araki Hiroyuki (1924–99). During a college

English class, Araki asked the students to translate a rather simple Japanese sentence into English—*Otōto to kawarimasu* (I'll put my brother on, or more literally, I'll replace myself with my brother)—which is commonly used on the telephone. Most of the students couldn't finish the sentence. This was due, he speculates, to the fact that they all began their English translation with "I will change...," but couldn't get beyond that point. That is to say, they tried to translate the intransitive *kawarimasu* (someone changes) as the transitive verb *kaemasu* (change someone), so they unconsciously, on the model of "the weather changes," translated the expression *otōto to kawarimasu* (replace my brother with someone) as if it were *otōto ni kawarimasu* (change [into] my brother). Obviously, they are using the formula *onozukara kawarimasu* (spontaneously change) when they should be using the *mizukara kaemasu* (intentionally replace).

Mizukara = Onozukara

Various issues can be pointed out concerning words like this and this way of thinking. To begin with, one familiar example is the "I novel" (*watakushi shōsetsu*), a style of confessional novel written by Naturalist writers following the notion that total exposure of what has happened *mizukara* around them, that is, around the protagonist "I," will naturally turn into a novel *onozukara*.

Following this notion, they attempted a total divulgence of themselves under the motto "Be truthful, be natural." However, when this approach was later accused of being contradictory, the novelist Tayama Katai (1872–1930) exclaimed, "It is not a contradiction or anything of the sort. The contradiction, the unprincipled behavior, cannot be helped because it is a fact. A fact! A fact!" (*Futon* [The Quilt]). And further, "As for the contemptibility of human beings ... this is what it means to be human. This is nature" ("Sei" [Life]). In this, there is no one responsible for what occurs. We are forced to conclude that this kind of naturalism has been reduced to self-justification or an unconditional acceptance of reality.

However, we cannot completely reject Naturalist literature, which was, in a sense, the expression of a certain honesty in modern Japan. The central issue is that this kind of literature was written and read because we harbor such notions within ourselves. Going back to the earlier example, if the phrase "it turns out that we will get married" is intended to mean, "This just happened to turn out that way," we can also say, "it turns out that we will get divorced" if our marriage does not go well and we decide to separate. There is no one responsible for the outcome.

This notion is implicitly based on the premise of the oneness and continuity between *mizukara* and *onozukara*, the self and Nature, and eventually the self and others. Needless to say, this state of affairs has been criticized as *amae* (dependence), *mugen hōyō* (infinite tolerance), *musekinin no taikei* (a system of irresponsibility).

Mizukara ≠ *Onozukara*

The relationship between *mizukara* and *onozukara* is not limited to this one aspect. While the expression "it turns out that we will get married" can be considered as mere self-justification without anyone responsible, it can also be seen as an expression of sensitivity to events beyond *mizukara*—the situation that resulted in marriage, various subsequent happy and unhappy events, other people's help, as well as forces at work in places where *mizukara* cannot reach.

Much excellent thought that is worthy of the name has been created by straining sensitivity to its limit and critiquing the previously mentioned Naturalist mode that Japanese thinking tends to fall into. As an example, I would like to take up the thought of the Buddhist priest Shinran (1173–1262) in relation to Naturalism. Shinran's teachings are often regarded as being analogous to Naturalism. Indeed, Shinran teaches that the absolute power of Amida (Amitabha) Buddha will help us even when we realize the hopelessness of our earthly desires. According to Shinran, Amida, as an object of belief by which we are saved, is indeed a function of *jinen* (自然), that is, *onozukara*.

While this way of thinking certainly resembles that of the Naturalists, and indeed shares many things in common, the crucial difference between the two is that Shinran never regarded our *mizukara* acts as overlapping with the *onozukara* function of Amida Buddha. In Naturalist literature, *mizukara* and *onozukara* are basically regarded as a continuum, but in Shinran's thought, *mizukara* acts are regarded as those of self-reliance (*jiriki*), whereas *onozukara* functions are always those involving outside help (*tariki*), or the absolute power of the Other, the Absolute Other (*zettai tariki*). It is crucial in Shinran's thought that this *onozukara* (Amida Buddha) exists as a force or function of the Absolute Other, from which is derived the immense difficulty of belief in the basically incomprehensible Absolute Other.

Mizukara = ≠ Onozukara

The discussion above can be put into perspective by referring to the work of the philosopher Kiyozawa Manshi (1863–1903).

Kiyozawa Manshi was a priest of Shin Buddhism in the Meiji period who attempted to shed new light on the *Tannishō* (Lamentations of Divergences), a 13th-century text attributed to a disciple of Shinran. Kiyozawa was also a serious student of Western philosophy. Using the terms *mugen* (infinite/infinity) and *yūgen* (finite/finitude), he poses the following questions: Do we human beings live as *yūgen* beings? If there is something *mugen* at all about us, are the two—*yūgen* and *mugen*—the same thing or two separate things? If they are separate things, it follows that *yūgen* is outside *mugen*, but this is contrary to the concept of *mugen*. Therefore, there cannot be *yūgen* outside *mugen*. In other words, *mugen* and *yūgen* must be the same body, or one body.

On the one hand, the first deduction is based on a *mugen* perspective. However, if seen from the point of view of *yūgen*, that is, our perspective, *yūgen* cannot be the same as *mugen* because *yūgen* has a boundary or limitation. Accordingly, if there is such a thing as *mugen*, the body of *mugen* must be outside *yūgen*. He writes:

> We should not overlook the fact that *mugen* and *yūgen* are of the same body, and that at the same time *mugen* exists outside *yūgen*.
>
> (*Tariki-mon tetsugaku gaikotsu shikō*
> [An Effort to Outline a Philosophy that Leads to the Other Power])

In Kiyozawa's argument, *yūgen* and *mugen* can be directly replaced with the terms *mizukara* and *onozukara*. When seen from the *onozukara* side, our *mizukara* is within it; however, when seen from the *mizukara* side, *onozukara* is absolutely outside, or alien.

Also related to this problem is the theory of "absolutely contradictory self-identity" proposed by the philosopher Nishida Kitarō (1870–1945), a notion that the two (the past and the future) are absolutely contradictory but essentially one, deriving ultimately from the same origin. This is connected to the relationship between *nasu* (act) and *naru* (emerge or turn out) put forward by Miki Kiyoshi, who was a disciple of Nishida. This issue is not discussed further here, but it should be noted that the complicated and important idea that *mizukara* is both within and without *onozukara* was brought up by Kiyozawa, Nishida, and Shinran.

The matter of the shifting boundary (*awai*) between *mizukara* and *onozukara*—that is, that *mizukara* is *onozukara* but at the same time not *onozukara*—is also a universal issue involving the *awai* between man and Nature, in that the self of man is Nature and at the same time not. *Awai* is a particularly Japanese ideological expression, but of course the issue itself is not confined to Japanese thought. In applied ethics, including bioethics and environmental ethics, the matter is now being widely discussed, and it is fair to say that it is being raised in cutting-edge science and technology as correlational issues in terms of where the *onozukara* area ends and where the *mizukara* area begins.

"Man Is Still Sublime"

Getting back to our initial issue of modern nihilism, the sociologist Mita Munesuke (b. 1937) addresses Karaki Junzō's proposal head-on in his "Sekai o shōgon suru shisō" (Thinking that Sublimates the World), included in his book *Gendai Nihon no kankaku to shisō* (Thought and Sensibility in Modern Japan). This is one of the most attractive approaches to the nihilism that we are now facing.

> Just as the most extreme philosophical thought at the end of the preceding century propounded "the death of God," so the most extreme thought at the end of this [the 20th] century will be "the death of man."
>
> This notion emerges particularly in the immediate issues of nuclear energy and environmental destruction. But it is also felt in many other ways, with the younger generations encountering many of them in their everyday lives. If man overcomes the crises of **nuclear energy** and **environmental pollution** and survives, he will still be reduced to nothing in several hundreds of millions of years later. The way of thinking that seeks meaning in the future will ultimately fall into nihility.
>
> The situation at the end of the 20th century **reveals** this condition in a visible form.
>
> We are on the threshold of a time when we have to develop a new, strong philosophy based on the clear realization that the death of man is a reality, that the

"world" that now inhabits our consciousness will come to an end. [Words in bold are the author's.]

Thus Mita declares that the ultimate end of contemporary thought is "the death of man," "the death of mankind." This is clearly revealed in the issues of nuclear energy and environmental destruction, but he also points out that especially younger generations accept these scenarios in different ways. This is succinctly seen in the survey I mentioned earlier in which half of elementary school fifth- and sixth-graders and junior high school students thought that "mankind would become extinct during their life time." The way of thinking that seeks meaning in the future is the optimistic "prospective" stance of the modern grasp of things that prioritizes *hakadoru* or *hakaru*. He insists that this view of life will ultimately fall into nihility, and we will have to develop a new, robust philosophy based on the clear recognition that the world will end.

Mita's "thinking that will sublimate the world" is in direct response to a phrase used by the writer and mercury-poisoning activist Ishimure Michiko (1927–2018), "man is still sublime," which appeared in a magazine article and was placed in a context that started as follows:

> Will the day ever come when we can view the time flowing over mankind in the same way we view geological time? ("Umi wa mada hikari" [The Sea Still Shines])

That is, according to Mita, "Ishimure somehow senses that

'mankind' is already dead. Or she senses that man could die at any moment. She is trying to be present at the final moment of human life. She is trying to sublimate man." In line with this, Mita also says:

> What does it mean to really sublimate a dead person? It is not about adorning the outer body with flowers, but about having the **awareness** to shed light from within on the "flowers" that bloomed because of the person **who had lived**, or on the living colors of these flowers. This is the way Ishimure concretely sublimated each of the deceased of Minamata in her works.
>
> This same approach is also the way to sublimate the **living**, that is, to awaken the flowers that are **already** blooming within the body of the living and to provide the vital **spark** of reality. The perception of "being sublime" is the only way to enliven the **living** as it is the only way to enliven the dead. Like the brightness of the sun dancing in the hollow caves of the mortal world, this way of thought brightens from within the whole world and its throngs of individual objects. [Words in bold are the author's.]
>
> ("Thinking that Sublimates the World")

Shōgon (to sublimate) was originally a word that meant to adorn a "buddha" (that is, the deceased) with flowers. Here it is construed to mean to enlighten each of the living (those who are living now but will eventually die, or who are felt to be already dead) and the world crowded with them. In this sense, "thoughts to sublimate the world" truly appears to be a proposal that can provide an answer to the present-day nihilism that plays with the notion of "the end of the world," indicating an unmistakable direction forward.

Elsewhere Mita (writing under the name Maki Yūsuke) says much the same thing in reference to the transformation of *shikisokuzekū kūsokuzeshiki* (色即是空空即是色; form is emptiness; emptiness is form):

> As long as we see the meaning of our acts and relations only as a resultant "product," the outcome of our lives and the whole history of mankind is death. The most we can do is to disrupt the existence of a few orbiting entities in the eternal darkness of the universe. The only way to transcend this nihilism without the self-deception that comes from all religions is by fully and lucidly recognizing this fact.
>
> That is, precisely because our life is ephemeral, precisely because the whole history of mankind is ephemeral, we have no choice but to fully retrieve the intense feelings we once possessed for the here and now, for each and every action and relationship.
>
> ("Shikisokuzekū to kūsokuzeshiki: Tōtetsu no kiwami no tenkai" [Form Is Emptiness and Emptiness Is Form: Transformation of the Extreme Lucidity], in *Kiryū no naru oto* [The Sound of Airstreams])

While "Form Is Emptiness and Emptiness Is Form: Transformation of the Extreme Lucidity" presents a reversal of Karaki's unremitting pursuit of the *mujō*-ness of what is *mujō*, in fact this extremely well-known Buddhist logic from the Heart Sutra (Prajnaparamitahrdaya) is not necessarily easy to understand. "Form is emptiness and emptiness is form" can be interpreted as meaning, "Every form (*shiki*) has no entity (*kū*), but the real nature of *kū* is exactly the universal phenomenon." The problem is how to convert this phrase into living language and thought. As Karaki pointed out, it is important to reconsider familiar expressions whose specific meanings have been lost.

This has continually been required of Buddhism itself. Further, if we broaden our perspective a little, we see that this phenomenon is not necessarily limited to Buddhism; such reinterpretation has a universality that can be invariably found in some form or other in the best philosophical and religious thought that plumbs the roots of human existence. Our discussion here also centers on it. One of the issues we are considering—the *awai* (shifting boundary) between *mizukara* and *onozukara*—is linked to this way of thinking.

The *Shōgon* of *Mizukara* and *Onozukara*

The Noh drama, which has been continuously performed since the 14th century, often employs methods to project life through the eyes of the dead. It looks back on life from the time of death after several decades or several hundreds of years have passed. It yearns for what is not, reenacts the past, and reminisces about ineradicable feelings of days gone by. All this might take place in the dream of a traveling priest. In Mita Munesuke's words, this is to have "the **awareness** to shed light from within on the 'flowers' that bloomed because of the person **who had lived,** or on the living colors of these flowers"—that is, it is to *shōgon* (sublimate) the dead.

I would like to look further into this matter by citing a particular work, the Noh play *Obasute* [The Discarded Crone]. The story goes roughly as follows.

The ghost of an old woman, who died when abandoned to the elements, appears in front of a traveler who has come to Mt. Obasute to see the harvest moon. Her intent is to spend a few pleasurable moments with him. Under a moonlight so brilliant that one could confuse it with the Pure Land, the old woman dances an emotion-filled dance. Failing to find comfort, she says, "Even though I have seen the bright moon over Mt. Obasute in Sarashina, so famous for moon viewing, it could not bring me solace." The inconsolable ghost sentimentally recalls days gone by, but at dawn her figure becomes invisible to the traveler, who, thinking she is gone, leaves the mountain. The old woman is left alone. She has been abandoned once again.

> The woman was deserted and alone; the mountain was the same as before. Mt. Obasute! Mt. Obasute!
>
> *(Obasute)*

The piece ends here. In the magazine article "Obasute no kozetsu" (The Isolation of 'Obasute'), Sagara Tōru writes, "The loneliness of abandonment is regarded not just as a feeling of desolation but as something beyond the interpersonal sphere." Overwhelming isolation underlines the life and death of human beings—what the writer Sakaguchi Ango (1906-55) called "the absolute solitude contained in existence itself," as will be seen in Chapter 5. This play is luminous with cold beauty because the ghost of the old woman, seeking consolation not in mankind but vainly in the moon, persisted to the end. According to Noh scholar Masuda Shōzō (b. 1930), "Instead of returning from the world of the dead to the world of the living, she bypassed death and metamorphosed into another existence" (*Nō no hyōgen* [Expressions of Noh]).

The author of *Obasute* (Zeami Motokiyo; ca. 1363-1443), who ended the play with the quiet refrain "Mt. Obasute! Mt. Obasute!" sees the old woman as being far beyond the human world. On "the lonesome mountain, with the wind blowing hard and the clouds unrelenting," she was and is still there, as lonely as before—a vividly appealing scene. Masuda's *Expressions of Noh* supports this interpretation with the following comment:

> It was a great solitude that calmly flowed on like the movement of the universe, accepting everything as it is. With neither sentimentality nor resignation, everything is eliminated and she is sublimated to the perfect clarity of the "thing-in-itself." What strength of life!

Thus, while seeing time as flowing over mankind much like geological time, Masuda confirms the strength of life. This is also an expression of the sublimity (*shōgon*) of *kūsokuzeshiki* (emptiness is form).

From the perspective of salvation, there is no salvation here worthy of the name. However, on the other hand, it does not drag us into the abyss of despair, but rather affirms the strength of life. This "reversal" was only possible because solitude, despite its loneliness, was exactly "a great solitude that flowed emotionless like the movement of the universe," as Masuda remarks.

In other words, the existence and acts of *mizukara* converge into an image of the universe or Nature itself (*onozukara*), where mountains and the moon are as they are. It is as if *mizukara* is confined to a special corner (*ichigū*) of the universe, solitary and insular but also sublime (*shōgon*).

"Flower petals fall, but the flower endures."

The above is a quotation from the Buddhist philosopher Kaneko Daiei (1881–1976), a student of Kiyozawa Manshi. It is a perfect explanation of the Noh drama *Obasute*. I came across it in a work by Matsubara Taidō (1907–2009), *Hannya shingyō nyūmon* (Introduction to the Heart Sutra). The phrase suddenly occurred to Kaneko when he was grieving over the loss of a young grandchild. He explained that it was a sudden insight (*shōken*) that all things are empty, as in *shikisokuzekū kūsokuzeshiki*, using the metaphor of two lenses.

> The first lens is to pierce the transient. The second lens is the realization that the truth is an empty state.

> We are forced to see things in their true light through these two lenses.... *(Introduction to the Heart Sutra)*

A "flower" constitutes the two lenses of "form is emptiness; emptiness is form" as well as the brightness of sublimity and the colors on which light is shed.

How can we, in our own *mizukara*, possess such a "flower"? This is the question before us.

CHAPTER
2

What Is the Meaning of *Tōtoi*?

*I want to remember the deceased as
unique, irreplaceable individuals. This is
what I mean by "mourning."*

Tendō Arata

On Reason

This chapter will discuss the meaning of the adjective *tōtoi* (*tōtosa* as a noun; roughly meaning exalted, noble, precious), and in particular the significance of the phrase "the *tōtosa* of man."

To give a concrete example, when a student commits suicide, frequently a teacher is called upon to give a speech about the *tōtosa* of man or of life itself. The issue here is what the teacher should say. What exactly is *tōtoi* or precious about man? The answer seems obvious to us, something we already know intuitively. But in this day and age it seems that it has to be put into words once again.

According to the high-school textbook *Rinri* (Ethics), "the idea of human dignity—that is, the idea that each one of us is irreplaceable and deserves respect as a being endowed with reason—is the most fundamental concept of modern times." As propounded by Kant and other philosophers, human beings are regarded as having reason, and an entity with the autonomous ability to execute decisions is referred to as a person, in which absolute meaning or value is sought. The famous saying "for this reason a person should never be treated as a means but as an end" derives from this thought.

In general, all other textbooks follow the same narrative, with chapters titled "Respect for Man" or "The Dignity of Man." Needless to say, this is premised on a Western way of thinking, a Christian way of thought.

From the ancient Greek definition of man as a rational animal, and its subsequent development by Christianity and the Renaissance, comes the idea that "man, created in the likeness of God, is considered the only being to whom reason has been granted, and is therefore a special entity positioned between God and nature" (*Ethics*). However, this reason-based anthropocentric way of thinking was not accepted *tout court* in the Orient, including Japan, because the Greek *logos* and the Christian God did not exist there.

Of course, since Japan has successfully modernized under the banner of Westernization and become an advanced democratic country, it has partially accepted such ways of thinking, but as long as the underlying idea is the view of man set out above, it remains doubtful whether the Japanese people fully understand and accept the ideas of reason, democracy, or basic human rights. (The number of Japanese Christians is said to be less than one percent of the total population.)

On the other hand, when assessing terminal care from a clinical perspective, the discussion of what to do and how to do it in a *tōtoi* way is often conducted in Western, Christian terms without even noticing it, just as clinical charts were customarily written in German or English.

Japan passed the Act on Organ Transplantation after heated discussion more than ten years ago, but the number of transplant operations remained low. The number has recently increased since the passage of an amendment, but this also seems to be a reflection of our resistance to the Western concept of brain death (i.e., an individual who has lost the rational ability to think can be regarded as dead).

In a recent study by the National Institute of Public Health (2009), the proportion of those who regarded brain death as a reasonable diagnostic standard was forty-three percent in Japan compared to sixty to seventy-one percent in four Western countries. Here we can detect the reason behind the Japanese people's resistance to the idea that it is acceptable to transplant an organ from an individual who cannot think or be self-sufficient—strictly speaking, this applies not only to brain-dead persons, but also to Alzheimer's disease sufferers, infants and toddlers—because without reason they are no longer *tōtoi* beings. Recently, the idea of basing *tōtosa* solely on the ability to reason or think, or to act autonomously, is being questioned by modern medicine.

Also, even in the West, the debate on "what is a person" is being re-thought. I believe this may mean that the very anthropocentric way of thinking based on reason, as we discussed above, is being reconsidered.

On Mystery (with Particular Reference to Life)

In light of the foregoing discussion, I would now like to examine how Japanese people have responded to and accepted the idea of *tōtoi*.

In Japanese mythology as depicted by the 8th-century *Kojiki* (A Record of Ancient Matters), there is no creator god (who is said to be the source of *tōtosa* in Western Christianity).

> The names of the gods that came into being in the plain of high heaven when Heaven and Earth began were Ame no Minaka-nushi (the god ruling the center of Heaven), next Takami Musubi (the god creating the high Heaven), and next Kami Musubi (the god creating the gods).... When the Earth, in its infancy and like unto floating oil, drifting around medusa-like, gods sprouted up like reed shoots, who were... Next... And next ...
>
> (*Kojiki*)

The *Kojiki* states that when heaven and earth began, everything, including the various gods, "emerged" via the *onozukara* workings of nature, as indicated by the sprouting of reed shoots.

First of all, these mysterious workings are seen as being *tōtoi* in themselves. Motoori Norinaga, among others, described this phenomenon as *reimyō* (mysterious) based on his study of the *Kojiki*. Fukuzawa Yukichi expresses his view, which we have previously referred to, in the following manner: "The great mechanism of the universe and nature is so subtle and mysterious that everything on this earth, from man down to animals, plants, and specks of dust, evades comprehension."

In a more general way, this amounts to the following idea:

Understanding of the self as a natural occurrence

rather than as a creation is full of wonders. Self-occurrence, or natural occurrence, is itself mysterious and ethereal. The self cannot be violated by others because it occurs naturally and lives here, or it occurs naturally and lives there.

(Sagara Tōru, *Jinmei no sonchō* [Respect for Human Life])

Sagara thinks that each human being is full of wonders, mysterious and ethereal, because the individual is a natural occurrence rather than a creation. The self is not something that was made or created arbitrarily, but occurs naturally. In this sense, both the self and others are *tōtoi*.

The *tōtosa* found in the operation of *onozukara* is not necessarily limited to living things. It is true of everything "from man down to animals, plants, and specks of dust." The ancient Japanese believed that this world—created by "the momentum of continuous occurrence" (Maruyama Masao, 1914–96)—is full of gods, and if there is a rather thick forest, for example, a god of the forest lives there, or if there is a deep pond, there is a god of the pond.

That is, everything that is extraordinary, possesses exceptional virtue, and is awesome is considered a god, and the *yaoyorozu* of *yaoyorozu no kami* (myriads of gods) means that their number is infinitely large. The ancient Japanese believed this world to be teeming with gods.

Therefore, the scope of *tōtosa* is not necessarily limited to living things, but is particularly applied to natural occurrences or to life (*inochi*). The etymology of the word *inochi* is explained as follows:

> *Inochi*
>
> *I* is *iki* (breath) and *chi* is power. Therefore, the original meaning is "the momentum of breath." The ancients seem to have regarded the fundamental power of living as a function of invisible momentum.
>
> (*Iwanami Classical Dictionary*)

This view of *iki* as the momentum of breath evinces a universal way of thinking or feeling shared by other cultures. The etymology of "anima," "psyche," and "spirit" all include the meaning of breath. In any event, the classical Japanese word *inochi* is now used as follows, based on the original meaning:

> 1. The fundamental force that gives creatures life.
> 2. A lifetime.
> 3. A life span.
> 4. The most important thing. The one thing that can be depended on.
> 5. The tattooed character that a man and a woman in love engrave on their upper arms followed by the name of the beloved, such as *"Yoshi-sama inochi"* (Dear Yoshi, My Life), principally in red-light districts in early modern times as a sign of everlasting steadfastness.
>
> (*Daijirin* [Great Forest of Words dictionary])

That is, *inochi* means, principally, the lifetime of each living thing or a life span, the length of a life. At the same time, it means the fundamental force that gives creatures life and makes them uniquely what they are. Most importantly, there is an understanding that the individual life is not different from life as a great fundamental force.

"The most important thing" and "the only thing one can depend on" (#4) and *"Yoshi-sama inochi"* (#5) can be regarded as figurative uses of #1 in that they don't relate to the individual self but to the force that makes things what they are. The *Great Forest of Words* cites *inochi no onjin* (life saver) and *inochi o sasageru* (offer up one's life) as examples.

Next we will look at two kanji for writing *inochi*: 生 and 命.

生 ᄽ ᄿ ᄾ

This character represents vegetation sprouting from the ground and means "live," "come into being," or "life."

命

This character is composed of 口 (mouth) and the component 令, the latter which indicates the pronunciation of the character and the sense of taking a person into service, with the overall meaning of ordering a person to do something. Also, based on the concept of the mandate of heaven, it is used to signify the course of events of the world or the "life" of a person.

(*Shinjigen* [New Font of Words])

Whereas 生 is an ideograph depicting vegetation sprouting from the ground, meaning "live" or "come into being," 命 is significantly found in the kanji compound 命令 (*meirei*; order). That is, the combination of the two into 生命 (*seimei*; life) is taken to mean that our life is given by the order of Heaven or something similar.

Based on the thought of Nishida Kitarō, the psychopathologist Kimura Bin (b. 1931) explains with a simple analogy the relationship between *onozukara* working at the root of our being and the *mizukara* of each of us individually:

> Let us imagine a fountain spouting water from a source under the full pressure of living spontaneity via exits that are individually separate. The curve of the water forming an arch according to the features of each exit would be the individual self. If we stand at the water's source and observe the movement before the water goes out the exit, we will see *onozukara*, and the water movement after exiting would be *mizukara*.
>
> (*Aida* [In-Between Space])

This analogy illustrates that the individual *mizukara* is pushed out under the pressure of *onozukara*. *Mizukara* is brought into existence by *onozukara*.

Mizukara, as expressed in the curving arch of the water, comes out of the exit differently according to the position, size, or length of the given exit. If the exit is in a high place, the water is not under so much pressure and does not go far, whereas if the exit is narrow, the water is small in quantity but goes far.

More specifically, this is an issue of objectively given conditions—for example, whether we are born as Japanese, male, or tall. It is a result of the function of *onozukara* as the absolute other, and in this regard *mizukara* is born as its absolute passivity. This analogy overlaps the etymology of *inochi* as something pushed out by the invisible fundamental force of "the momentum of breath" as well as the origin of *seimei* signifying a state of being kept alive by a certain outside directive. Coming back to *tōtosa*, there is a poem that is attributed to the Buddhist monk and poet Saigyō (1118–90):

> I do not know what is here,
> But my eyes water
> Because I feel so blessed.

Saigyō apparently penned this when visiting the sacred Shinto shrine Ise Jingū. When there, Saigyō suddenly began to shed tears without any particular reason. I think this poem fully expresses the religious feelings of Japanese about the subtle and mysterious wonder of *onozukara*.

In a survey of religious consciousness, less than twenty percent of Japanese people replied in the affirmative when asked, "Do you believe in something?" However, when asked "Do you have a religious mind?" almost eighty percent replied in the affirmative. Indeed, some eighty million Japanese people are said to pay a visit to a shrine or temple every New Year's. During Obon (the Festival of the Dead held around mid-August) there is likewise a huge movement of people returning to their ancestral homes or to visit the family grave, and even including those who go for personal reasons, there is a great folk migration that takes place. There is an unusually high level of religious energy in these moments, and what mobilizes it is the topic we are addressing here.

In the New Year's visits, people go to a nearby Shinto shrine or Buddhist temple, not really caring which it is. The way of worship does not differ greatly between the two religions. At either place people simply make a wish for something. They say a prayer, not knowing "what is here." It is as if they are praying to the subtle and mysterious workings of *onozukara*.

On Activeness

The *tōtosa* of what occurs naturally has been reinforced by Shintoist animism and the Buddhist concept of the transmigration of souls, or fate. This is why there is a feeling of *tōtosa* toward every living thing, as opposed to the Western Christian concept of anthropocentrism, although the privileged state of human life is also always recognized in Japan.

Kimura's water fountain metaphor, where an arch of *mizukara* is pushed out under the pressure of *onozukara*, is not necessarily limited to human beings, but is true to the specific conditions of the *onozukara* and *mizukara* of every creature.

However, especially in the case of human beings, they can change the form of the exits with their own will or effort. They can enlarge or plug it. Then, the curve of the arch has naturally to change. Consideration of this point is related to the issue of the *awai* (shifting boundary) between the *onozukara* and *mizukara*.

Here I would like to make use of Sagara Tōru's concept of *onozukara keijijōgaku* (*onozukara* metaphysics) to support this discussion.

> Our ideological tradition has respected everything from human beings to other worldly things as "natural occurrences." However, we probably perceived an imperturbable absolute in the existence of each human being because we saw a mysterious activeness in that human beings, in accordance with the reality they face, live *mizukara* in a state of *onozukara*.
>
> (*Nihon shisō no naka no ningen no songen ni tsuite* [Human Dignity as Found in Japanese Thought])

In the tradition of Japanese thought all things are respected as natural occurrences, but different from plants and other animals, human beings have a certain privilege in that they do not accept the *onozukara* environment as it is.

This is a perception that a certain dignity lies in the "mysterious activeness" of *mizukara* as it unfolds vis-à-vis reality, without accepting the workings of *onozukara* as is.

For example, Japanese views of mankind from the medieval period to the early modern and modern periods include:

> "Man is the soul of heaven and earth."
> (Yoshida Kenkō, 1284–1350, *Tsurezuregusa* [Essays in Idleness])

> "Generally, Man receives the virtues of heaven and earth and is born with the five Confucian virtues [benevolence, justice, courtesy, wisdom, and sincer-

ity]... Therefore Man can be referred to as the soul of all things."

(Kaibara Ekken, 1630–1714, *Wazoku dōjikun*
[A Guide to Japanese Customs for Children])

"With the functions of mind and body as the soul of all things, Man commands everything between heaven and earth."

(Fukuzawa Yukichi, *Gakumon no susume*
[Encouragement of Learning])

Although such views became conspicuous from the medieval period on, the phrase "the soul of all things" (or the lord of all things) is first found in Chinese ancient literature, including the *Shu ching* (The Book of History).

However, this is somewhat different from the Western notions of reason and autonomy as seen earlier. We will go into detail about this point later, but for the moment the Japanese concept can be correctly allegorized as follows:

> The path of humanity is like a waterwheel. Half of it follows the water current, and the other half turns against the current. If the waterwheel is entirely within the water, it does not turn and will be swept away. On the other hand, it cannot move away from the water.

(Ninomiya Sontoku, *Ninomiya-ō yawa*
[Night Chats with Old Man Ninomiya])

Thus, mankind is likened to a waterwheel, which only turns by half following the water current and half going against it. The water current means the *onozukara* function, which the *mizukara* function does not fully follow nor get away from or unilaterally control, but operates in the shifting boundary (*awai*) in between.

At any rate, it seems important that *tōtosa* has been perceived proactively, in that rather than accepting *onozukara* as it is, *mizukara* has the ability to act on *onozukara*. This issue will be taken up again in Chapter 5 in the discussion of the *awai* between *onozukara* and *mizukara*.

Ichigū-ness

I will now look more closely at my view of *tōtosa*, making use of the passage excerpted previously from Shiga Naoya's essay "A Drop in the Nile," which I will quote again here for convenience sake.

> It is beyond our imagination how many million years have passed since man came into being, and in that passage of time countless people were born, lived, and died. I was born as one of them and am now living, but I am as a drop in the grandly flowing Nile, the only drop that is me for all time; even if you go back scores of thousands of years, you cannot find another me, and even though scores of thousands of years pass, I will not be born again. Still, I am a drop in a mighty river, which is sufficient.

I would like to reconfirm that two kinds of self-perception are dealt with here. One is the recognition that I am just a drop of water in the grandly flowing Nile. The other is the recognition that this mere drop is a drop that is me for all time, that is, it is a once and only occurrence.

Each of these two types of self-recognition expresses the *tōtosa* of the *mizukara* existence.

The first leads to the notion of *ichigū* (a special "corner" of the universe), mentioned above. The notion that I am a drop in the Nile is not a mere relative perception. The drop may be nothing but a drop, but it does not simply appear from nothingness and disappear into nothingness; rather it is a drop of a grandly flowing mighty river. The perception is of a drop of water emerging from the mighty river and going back to the grand flow again. As such, the drop is by no means empty of value but is seen as something meaningful and *tōtoi* in itself.

Shiga relates the following about his trip to the Kinosaki hot springs for its medicinal value when he was nearing death:

> One morning I saw a dead bee on the roof… It had been there for three days or so. As I looked at it, it gave me a feeling of quiet peace. It was also sad. It was sad to see the dead bee's body left on the cold roof tile at the close of the day, when the other bees had gone into the hive. At the same time, it was so very quiet.
>
> During the night a heavy rain fell. The next morning the weather cleared, and the leaves of the trees, the ground, and the roof were washed clean. The dead

body of the bee was no longer there... I began to feel at home with the serene calm... Being alive and being dead were not opposites. There did not seem to be much difference between them.

(*Kinosaki nite* [At Kinosaki])

The familiarity with death that Shiga sensed through the death of the bee was derived from the discovery that our death is the same as that of a bee. That is, it comes from the perception that death is a natural event in the context of a larger nature, where being alive and being dead are not opposites and between which there is not much difference.

As I stated earlier, modern Japanese people have taken a particular interest in discussing life and death, including the notion that we will become *mu* (nullity) when we die. These ideas do not always come from modern science or materialism. Rather, they are expressed in contexts such as Shiga's.

The recognition that the bee and every other thing is a certain kind of *ichigū*-ness, only an instant in time, only a drop of water, but that they emerge from a grand *onozukara* and disappear into it again, is itself an important view of life and death and the universe. There is in it a sense of *tōtoi*.

Once-ness: Being a One and Only

Another theme in the self-recognition of "A Drop in the Nile" is the absoluteness of being a drop of water or a "corner" (*ichigū*) of something grand and at the same time as being oneself. This is the recognition of "I," which is "the only drop that is me for all time; even if you go back scores of thousands of years, you cannot find another me, and even though scores of thousands of years pass, I will not be born again." This is the absolute recognition that "I" am a one-time-only, unique existence. The phrase used to express this is *kakegae ga (no) nai*, where *kakegae* means "replacement" and *ga (no) nai* means "does not exist")—that is, there is nothing that can be used as a substitute; I am irreplaceable. This *kakegae-no-nai* feeling is composed of various elements, but the underlying fact is that the "I" inhabiting this particular body lives and dies as a one-time-only, unique existence.

Modern science shows us that the genome or DNA of each person is different. No two living things are exactly the same in this world. DNA analysis is based on this fact. Of course, regarding the genome, it is also true that other living creatures share a significant portion of our genetic material. For example, humans and chimpanzees share more than ninety-eight percent of the same genome, with only a one or two percent difference.

That is, as concerns the *onozukara*, they overlap each other almost entirely, but a slight difference creates a human being and, in particular, each individual "I."

The idea that to be alive is an irreplaceable, one-time-only event is ages-old, but it has been especially in modern times that "I" began to be regarded as an absolute entity called "the modern self."

It took Shiga ten years to revise and rewrite "A Drop in the Nile." The initial text read, "No matter how many years pass I will not be born again. [signed] Naoya." Then he deleted his signature and added: "Still, I am but a drop in a mighty river, which is sufficient." (Sudō Matsuo, *Shiga Naoya no shizen* [Nature in Shiga Naoya])

Shiga turned from the perception of one-time-only uniqueness to the perception of *ichigū*-ness as a special "corner" of the universe, and tried to come to the understanding that "it is sufficient" that one-time-only uniqueness and *ichigū*-ness are out of synchronization, though they do overlap as self-recognition. In accordance with this overlapping and misalignment, the feeling of *tōtosa* slightly changes. This issue leads directly to the matter of "rarity," which will be discussed below.

Unusualness (Gratitude) 1 (Fate)

As every form in this world is fleeting, what has existed in one instant perishes in the next, and various things emerge anew in the world. It is similar to a variety of clouds taking shape in what was until then a clear blue sky... Though a transient being, you did not come into this world without meaning. Through a myriad of different causes and conditions meeting together, you have come into this world. You were born for a reason. This gives us a sense of wonder... Yes, it is no exaggeration to say that you, who are living now, are a kind of miracle. Your existence is really and truly *arigatai* (something to be grateful for). Actually, your life is simply a drop in the grand river of the universe. Only a drop, but without this drop, the river of the universe does not come into existence. Your life swiftly flows in this river. The grand river of the universe swiftly flows in your life. That is, you are the universe itself.

(Arai Man, *Jiyūyaku hannya shingyō* [The Heart Sutra: A Free Translation])

The above is an excerpt of a loose translation of the *Heart Sutra* by the multitalented Arai Man (b. 1946), which, in light of Shiga's "A Drop in the Nile," implies much more.

This excerpt corresponds to the *shikisokuzekū kūsokuzeshiki* (form is emptiness; emptiness is form) section of the *Heart Sutra*. All the forms in this world exist only for a fleeting moment, like clouds that come and go in the vault of heaven. Everything is protean; people are born and die. However, each being has come into existence out of innumerable different causes and conditions, and each person is a "miraculous being," a "being that is grounds for gratitude" that has "meaning." He explains that a "drop" in the swift-flowing grand river of the universe implies that the river does not exist without the gathering of the drops.

Every blade of grass needs a certain amount of soil, water, and nutrients, and above ground it needs to take in sunlight and carbon dioxide and expel oxygen. The soil, water, and nutrients, which originally existed in different forms, have come to be as they are. The oxygen that the grass exudes is taken in by other animals, and the grass itself will be eaten by other animals, or will decay into nutrients or soil. As this cycle is expanded, it eventually leads to the whole grand river of the universe.

To give another simple illustration, whenever a certain "you" exists, this "you" always has a father and mother, and the father and mother have parents, the grandparents of "you." The grandfather and grandmother have parents, your great-grandparents. Therefore, if we go back two generations, there are four ancestors ($=2^2$); in the case of three generations back, there are 8 ($=2^3$); in case of four generations back, 16 ($=2^4$); in the case of 10 generations back, 1,024 ($=2^{10}$); and in the case of 20 generations back, 1,048,576 ($=2^{20}$). Twenty generations back means only 400 to 500 years ago, but during that period there were as many as one million people who were your potential ancestors, meeting each other on various occasions, experiencing many events, getting married and starting families, and then their children proceeding to have similar encounters. These events were repeated by each generation, and the last cycle led to the present "you." If any of 64 people, or 32 pairs six generations earlier, had broken up and had not married, or if they had married but did not have a child, who would be the ancestor of "you"? "You," of course, would not be here.

Just a simple thought experiment reveals that numerous encounters and events had to come together for "you" to exist. You have indeed come into being out of innumerable different causes and conditions.

This argument takes into account only the spread of parents and children in the human species, but in fact "you" are now alive because you have eaten and ingested a myriad of other *inochi* (lives), and the numerous *inochi* were there because they had eaten and taken in a myriad of other *inochi*. This linkage spreads out immeasurably. "You," who has come into this world through a myriad of different causes and conditions, is the culmination of the chain of myriad *inochi*. If the history of life on earth covers 3.5 billion years, "you," as a drop of water, are at the forefront of the swift flow of living things with a history of 3.5 billion years.

One of the teachings in the *Kegonkyō* (*Avatamasaka Sutra*) is *jūjū mujin* (more and more, without limit), which means that everything is part of a string of life, where each life is inexhaustibly overlapped and conditioned by other lives. This means that if one thing happens, all other things will be linked to it as its cause or result. To "come into being out of numerous different causes and conditions" is also *jūjū mujin*.

The same is equally true of grass, trees, and animals, but Buddhism teaches us that coming into this world as a human being is a cause for thanks (*arigatai*), a precious event amounting to a miracle.

> It is difficult to receive life as a human, and even though you will die in the end, you should be grateful to be alive now. (*Dhammapada*)

Another sutra (*Samyukta Agama*) explains this by means of an analogy known as "the blind turtle and the driftwood." Imagine that a blind turtle living on the sea floor rises to the surface once every 100 years. On the surface of the water is a piece of driftwood with a hole in it. The probability of being born a human being is less than the turtle's chances of surfacing precisely so its head fits in the hole. Another literary work states that it is as difficult to be born in a human body as it is to find a needle in the ocean or stand on the summit of a high mountain and put a thread through the eye of a needle at its foot. (Saichō, *Ganmon* [A Prayer])

Therefore, Buddhism teaches that we should undergo religious training and achieve enlightenment while we are alive as human beings. On the other hand, there is a long succession of numerous coincidences behind the fact that we have been born as a human, as a "I" who exists here and now. This is a cause for thanks (*arigatai*) in the context of the difficulty of its being realized as well as *arigatai* in the context of *tōtoi*. "Your existence is really and truly *arigatai*."

Unusualness (Gratitude) 2 (Time)

As explained above, *tōtosa* as unusualness sheds light on people's fate or history that results from numerous different causes and conditions, but it can also be regarded as the temporal unusualness of being.

Tōtosa is intrinsic to the short period we enjoy as human beings, which is described in Arai's free translation as a fleeting existence.

The writer Inoue Yasushi (1907–91) wrote the following poem titled "Jinsei" (Human Life):

> Opening a page of the book *Genesis of the Earth* by Dr. M., I explained it to my child in simple terms:
>
> "Physicists concluded, based on calculating geothermal heat, that the history of the earth was from 20–40 million years old. However, later on, geologists proposed a figure of 87 million years based on the salt content of seawater, or 330 million years in light of the principle of the generation of aqueous rocks. On the

other hand, more recent scientists have announced, in the discourse on radioactivity, that the oldest rock on earth is 1.4 or 1.6 billion years old. In the present age of nuclear energy, the secret of the age of the earth may be further expanded with additional astounding figures. However, the recorded history of human life is only 5,000 years, and the history of the Japanese people is less than 3,000. A human life is said to be 50 years. Father is 40 years old, and you are less than 13."

Suddenly, I stopped speaking. It was because I was struck by a love of life in the simplest and purest form ever.

("Jinsei" [Human Life], *Kitaguni* [The Northern Land])

Near the end of the novel *Migomori no umi* (A Lake to Hide In) by Hata Kōhei (b. 1935), there is an interesting passage. The scene is a radio program on which a renowned scientist says, "Suppose just a year, or 365 days, have passed since the birth of the earth. Then, when was mankind born during the past one year?" Hearing that the answer was "on the last day of the year, at 11:59:30 p.m.," the main character speaks movingly as follows:

> "The history of mankind is only 30 seconds compared to one year of the history of the earth. Our culture of the past 50 centuries is less than one second. Makiko casually thought that the face of Kōda Michiko, which suddenly crossed her mind, was a face that could accept the solitude of less than one second without

any astonishment. Kōda, and probably her sister Kikuko too, know the exact weight and lightness of this one or two seconds, and on this particular point we three resigned ourselves to the anguish of life and death, and were united with Kōda's so-called 'kindred spirits'... They regarded with suspicion any judgment or act conceived in the belief of the future of mankind; they trusted in a totally different eternity, that is, the mystery of instantly converting one second, one moment, into eternity. They are the kind of people who bravely abandon politics, culture, ideology, or any action that is not based on loneliness as the solid gold of fleeting life, and who keep suffering in order to sneak a look into the mystery within the minds of familiar, select people." (*A Lake to Hide In*)

Not only life but the whole of human history is dismissed as something less than thirty seconds old, and politics, culture and ideology are less than one second, compared with one year of the history of the earth. In Hata's fictional world a trust in the mysterious ability to transform one second, one moment, into eternity emerges when the character accepts the solitude of less than one second without astonishment.

Loneliness as the solid gold of fleeting life seems to be of the same quality as Inoue Yasushi's "love of life in the simplest and purest form ever."

Yoshida Kenkō's 14th-century *Essays in Idleness* outlines the idea of the preciousness, the difficulty, or the *arigatai* nature of existence itself, rather than regarding it as too short or too small relative to something else:

> It is wrong to say that summer does not come until the spring is gone, and that autumn does not begin until summer is over. Spring gradually prepares the air of summer; the feeling of autumn is already there in summer; autumn is already chilly; October has Indian summer days… Death does not come from ahead, but is now looming from behind… The end of life comes unexpectedly. It is a precious wonder that we have escaped death up to today.

Summer does not come after spring ends. Autumn does not come after summer ends. There is already a sign of autumn during summer, which gradually grows and becomes autumn before we notice it. There is the word *koharu* ("small spring"), which refers to a warm winter day. When *koharu* grows larger, it becomes a big spring, and it is then we realize that spring has come. This is how the seasons go round. Kenkō, based on his observation of the transition of the seasons, says that it is also true of human birth and death, or the four inevitable stages of mankind—birth, aging, sickness, and death.

In other words, death does not begin after life is over, but death is already beginning within life. "Death does not come from ahead, but is now looming from behind." We will die someday, but death is not in the future but already clinging to our backs. He also says that we are rapidly melting like a snowman on a spring day. We may die at any moment; therefore, it is itself a "precious wonder" that we have survived until today.

This is the same argument as that of the *Dhammapada*, which says that "even though you will die in the end, you should be grateful to be alive now," which follows the words: "It is difficult to receive life as a human being."

The *Dhammapada* then goes on to urge us to enjoy being here and now as an *arigatai* rarity.

> If we were to live in this world forever, as if the dew on Adashino never vanished or the smoke from Mt. Toribe never ceased, there would be no feeling of *aware* (pity). The world is wonderful because it is uncertain… If you are never satisfied and regret death, life would be like a night's dream even though you lived a thousand years.

Both Adashino and Mt. Toribe are the names of places in Kyoto. Adashino was the site of a burial ground, Mt. Toribe that of a crematorium. The fact that the smoke from Mt. Toribe never ceased implies that people were dying every day. If dew did not vanish from the graves, if smoke ceased to rise from the crematorium, or if human beings did not die, we would never have feelings of *aware*, that is, sentiments or feelings of pity.

The word *aware* was originally an exclamation somewhat similar to "oh my." Whatever makes us sigh in this way is *aware*. This feeling emerges because the world is *mujō* or *hakanai*. The world is "wonderful"—interesting, meaningful, and diverting—

because it is uncertain. If we want more and more, are not satisfied and lose any sense of pity, life will pass like a single night's dream even though a thousand years have gone by.

As we saw in Chapter 1, we should retrieve the irreplaceable *tōtosa* of the present moment, which is devoid of calculation (*hakaru*) and the seeking of results in the future. In this, we have seen that the notion of *hakanai* is of utmost importance in being able to know *tōtosa*.

Shikisokuzekū Kūsokuzeshiki

The two kinds of *tōtosa* of unusualness cannot, of course, be distinctly differentiated, and both possess, as Arai's interpretation shows, the unusualness found in the logic of *shikisokuzekū kūsokuzeshiki* (form is emptiness; emptiness is form). The following is a passage from Mita's work I cited in the previous chapter, but here I would like to quote from a different part of that work to explain his conception of *shikisokuzekū*:

> Even when all value becomes empty, there is one value, however, that comes vividly to life. The best part of Buddhism, I believe, consists in a feeling about the value of all creation that surfaces when we see all creation as empty. The dialectical transposition of *shikisokuzekū kūsokuzeshiki* completely encompasses the truth of the relationship between human beings and the world....
>
> That is, precisely because our life is ephemeral,

precisely because the whole history of mankind is transient, we must retrieve, in the here and now, the sense of life-giving preciousness of each act and relationship.

("Form Is Emptiness and Emptiness Is Form: Transformation of the Extreme Lucidity")

Mita tells us to fully retrieve the sense of preciousness of each act or relationship in the here and now, which emerges when we clearly realize that our lives are fleeting and that the whole history of mankind is transient. Here, "form is emptiness; emptiness is form" is considered as a dialectic of transposition from the recognition of the emptiness of all creation to a recognition of the value of all creation. "Emptiness is form" is perceived as indicating life-giving preciousness.

"Preciousness" is, of course, directed toward the existence of the self, but at the same time it exists as the preciousness of each act and relationship in the here and now. Both acts and relationships are within the realm embracing the self and others, which shows that the *tōtosa* found there is born and felt as a relationship rather than being isolated.

Relationality (the Soul [*Tamashii*])

I would like to move on from the issue of *tōtosa* of unusualness to the issue of *tōtosa* in relationality.

Nakahara Chūya (1907–37) wrote a poem titled "Tsukiyo no hamabe" (The Beach on a Moonlit Night):

> One moonlit night a button was lying at the water's edge.
>
> I picked it up without thinking why, with no intention of putting it to use,
>
> but for some reason I couldn't throw it away and put it in my pocket.
>
> One moonlit night a button was lying at the water's edge.
>
> I picked it up without thinking why, with no intention of putting it to use,
>
> but I couldn't bring myself to throw it at the moon;
> I couldn't bring myself to throw it at the waves.
> So I put it in my pocket.
>
> The button I picked up on a moonlit night touched my fingertips and touched my heart.
>
> The button I picked up on a moonlit night, how could I throw it away?

Chūya wrote this after the death of his two-year-old son. In the poem his son is likened to a button. The button does not have any inherent value. He hesitates to throw it away not because it possesses reason, active life, spirituality, or any such intrinsic value. He did not intend to use it for some purpose. Still, he could not throw it away. Although the button was just something he picked up on the beach, his picking it up represented a definite encounter between him and the button. From a relationship that began by chance, the button became something irreplaceable (*kakegae-no-nai*) and *tōtoi*.

I came across this poem in the book *Kotoba no chikara, ikiru chikara* (The Power of Words, the Power to Live) by Yanagida Kunio (1875-1962). He had also lost a son, and thereafter developed his own "medical science of death" through his relationship with his deceased son. Yanagida says:

> The spiritual life of a person does not end with death. The everlasting life of that person, which is purified by departure (and worthy of being called a *tamashii* or soul), will keep living in the hearts of his family and friends. Also a wonderful thing happens when these people, who possess the living memory of their beloved one, receive the warm energy of life by continuing to speak of their everlasting recollections of the deceased.
>
> *("Jinsei no kotae" no dashikata*
> [How to Discover "the Answer to Human Life"])

Here the *tamashii* is seen as the purified everlasting life of that person, which comes through death. Someday I would like to discuss the issue of *tamashii* separately, but in any case Yanagida thinks that it will keep living in the heart of the deceased's family and friends.

On the other hand, Yanagida, in the same book, says, "in a profound sense of loss, as if in pursuit of my son and reconnoitering the landscape of the journey I will surely make one day myself, I got a copy of the sutra *Shushōgi* (Meaning of Methods and Purposes) and perused the *Heart Sutra*. The phrase *shikisokuzekū kūsokuzeshiki* struck me as if it were a self-evident truth." He continues:

> What was filling my heart was a feeling that *kū* is not absolute emptiness but space in which a purified spirit (exactly what should be called a soul) dwells, invisible to mortal eyes. It is different from heaven or paradise. It is not black cosmic space. I would venture to say that it is something that melds in with the landscape of the natural world....
>
> (*How to Discover "the Answer to Human Life"*)

Here we see that *tamashii* is regarded as a purified spirit invisible to mortal eyes and that the *kū* of *shikisokuzekū kūsokuzeshiki* is the space that such a purified spirit dwells in. This statement and the remark in the previous passage that the *tamashii* will keep living in the heart of the deceased's family and friends are obviously in different phases; however, it seems to me that these two issues should be considered together.

As we can see from the previous chapter, Kaneko Daiei's words—"Flower petals fall, but the flower endures. The form perishes, but the being endures"—leads to an understanding of *shikisokuzekū kūsokuzeshiki*.

All forms change, and as a physical substance flower petals fall, but the purified, everlasting life of the flower that has bloomed does not disappear: "The flower endures."

Even if we do not relate this to the Buddhist logic of *shikisokuzekū kūsokuzeshiki*, there is, for example, the French philosopher's remark:

> Death destroys all life, but it cannot nullify the fact

that we lived... Among that which we call reality, only the invisible, intangible, simple, and the seemingly incomprehensible metaphysical escapes nihility.

(Vladimir Jankélévitch, *La mort*,
from the Japanese translation by Nakazawa Norio)

That which is invisible, intangible, simple, metaphysical, and incomprehensible is also a form of reality. This is the state of Yanagida's purified spirit invisible to mortal eyes.

The point here is that, whether we are considering the "truth" that "the dialectical transposition of *shikisokuzekū kūsokuzeshiki* completely encompasses the truth of the relationship between human beings and the world," or whether we are considering the "reality" that we have lived and our lives cannot be nullified, it is important that this be stated not in an abstract manner but as a concrete flower blooming within those who are left behind. Moreover, this is the only way to demonstrate that the "flower endures."

Posing the question "What does it mean to really sublimate a dead person?" Mita answered that it was not "about adorning the outer body with flowers, but about having the **awareness** to shed light from within on the flowers that bloomed because of the person **who had lived**, or on the living colors of these flowers." We offer flowers at a funeral, and this is not only meant as an act to adorn the outer body, but also an act to "shed light from within" on the content of the person's life, or the color of his or her life. This is what to sublimate, or "the flowers that bloomed," means.

Itamu, Tomurau

Concurrently, this sublimating and blossoming also means *itamu* (to mourn) or *tomurau* (to condole). *Itamu* originally meant that our body or heart hurt for some reason. That is, *itamu* is based on a "painful" (*itai*) sensation caused by some injury to ourselves, and to mourn (*itamu*) a person's death signifies that our heart painfully feels the loss and mourns the passing of the deceased. According to the dictionary *New Font of Words*, the kanji used to write *itamu* (悼) is made up of 心 (heart) and 卓 (slip out), and refers to the sorrow that might come with a sudden "slippage" of vital energy.

The feeling of *itai* is not, however, confined to the individual self, but implies ethical possibilities that extend to compassion for the pain (*itami*) of other people, such as seen in the words *itamashii* (pitiful) and *itawashii* (heartbreaking), as well as to feelings of *itawaru* (care) for such people. Though implying broader meanings like this, the basic meaning of *itamu* remains that we ourselves feel pained (*itai*).

In his introduction to *Kokubungakushi kōwa* (*The History of Japanese Literature*) by the literary historian Fujioka Sakutarō (1870–1910), Nishida Kitarō wrote the following about the sorrow (*kanashimi*) of losing a beloved daughter, a tragedy he shared with Fujioka:

> The dead never come back to life, so they tell me to accept it and forget about her. However, for a parent this would be unbearable.... Somehow or other I want

to remember her. I want to leave some memorial to her. At the very least, I want to remember her while I am still alive. This is what it means to be a parent.... To remember her from time to time, from occasion to occasion, is the least I can do to alleviate my suffering and to care after the dead with all my heart. The anguish is truly tormenting, but the parent does not want the pain to go away.... However worthless a person might be, his or her spirit cannot be compensated by other things. The absolute value of a human life is most painfully felt when we have lost a child.... Why does a lovely child, who was talking, singing, and playing until just a moment ago, suddenly disappear, reduced to white bones in an urn? If this is life, life is absurd. A deep meaning must be there. The spiritual life of a human being is not so insignificant.

As we can see from this, it was the personal philosophy of Nishida to delve into the deeper meaning of the spiritual life of human beings. The death of Yūko, his second oldest daughter, happened three years before the publication of his first philosophical work, *Zen no kenkyū* (An Inquiry into the Good). Remembering her while he was still living was not only his way of alleviating his mental suffering as a parent but also a means of embracing the dead child as she was in his memory. No matter how painful it is, we can only bring the dead back to this world through the *itami* (pain) of living people.

To *itamu*—that is, to bring the dead into this world through *itami*—is an act that directly leads to the act of *tomurau*. *Tomurau* (written 弔う) means "to visit" or "to call on." It also means "to inquire about" (問う), that is, to recall the deceased's thoughts and feelings. At a wake or at the following memorial service, mourners recall and talk about what the deceased was like, what he said or what characteristics he had. *Tomurau* implies such meanings.

Traditional Noh drama has *tomurai* (the noun form of *tomurau*) and *itami* as one of its main themes. In much of its repertoire, the *shite* (protagonist) is the ghost of a person who died with overwhelming sorrow and pain, whom a priest as the *waki* (side character) visits. Here the haunted thoughts of the *shite* are heard and depicted. Through the *tomurai* and *itami* of the *waki*, the thoughts of the dead are understood by the audience and committed to memory. In doing so, the soul, flower, and other things important to the *shite* take shape. In the "flower petals fall, but the flower endures," this is what is meant by the "flower endures."

> "I want to remember the deceased as a unique existence who cannot be replaced by any other person. I call this *itamu*."

So says the protagonist of the novel *Itamu hito* (The Mourner) by Tendō Arata (b. 1960). What made him a mourner "was the feeling of guilt about forgetting the dead, which is so widespread in this world" and "the stabbing pain in my chest asking me if this is alright, is this as it should be." This seems to be the same feeling as that portrayed by Nishida and Noh.

Therefore, if there is no one to *tomurau* or *itamu*, the flower loses the space to bloom. It is often said that people die twice. First, a person dies physically, and second when people who *tomurau* and *itamu* that person pass from this earth, and the soul or flower disappears for at least those people. (However, even if scores or hundreds of years have passed, *tomurau* and *itamu* can culminate in a Noh drama, and flowers will bloom there again.) "Flower petals fall, but the flower endures" is an expression of such a relationship.

CHAPTER
3

Re-Visiting "Flower Petals Fall, but the Flower Endures"

The *nenbutsu* chanted after you have lost a parent will be different from the *nenbutsu* chanted before that event, containing something rich and powerful, though you are praying to the same Buddha.

Kaneko Daiei

The Direction of *Tomurai* and *Itami* in Miyazawa Kenji

In a previous book, *"Kanashimi" no tetsugaku* (The Philosophy of "Sorrow"), I considered the nature of Miyazawa Kenji's acts of *tomurai* and *itami* toward his sister Toshi, but a crucial issue remained unaddressed. I would like to review the process leading up to that issue.

After losing his beloved sister, Kenji wrote three poignant poems, including "Musei dōkoku" (Wailing Inaudibly), in which he silently cries out in sorrow (*kanashimi*) but has difficulty expressing himself in words. After these poems, he stopped writing for a while, emotionally paralyzed.

Half a year later, Kenji attempts to face up to Toshi's demise, something he had been unable to do before, and to "begin to consider" the fact of her death.

> I have to begin to consider
> what I must begin to consider.
> Toshi has gone in a way
> that people call death.
> I don't know where she has gone after that.

> This cannot be measured in terms of spatial direction.
> Everyone turns around in circles
> when they try to grasp this ungraspable direction.
>
> ("Aomori banka" [Aomori Lament])

To "begin to consider" means to *tomurau* and *itamu*, not to come to terms with what people generally call death. By doing so, he intended to fulfill his wish to make Toshi's flower bloom and to always have her at his side. To be more precise, he tried to accomplish this by writing a series of laments while traveling in Aomori, Hokkaido, and Okhotsk.

However, what became clear in the process was the proposition that emerged from Kenji's belief in the *Lotus Sutra*: namely, that since everything in this universe is linked, a beloved individual should not be separated from that linkage.

> "Since we are all brothers and sisters of old, we should
> not pray for a single individual alone."
> And I never did so.
> Night and day after she left
> I have never, I think, not even once, prayed that
> she alone should go to a better place.
>
> ("Aomori Lament")

We can see a quite delicate expression here. Certainly, Kenji did not pray that "she alone should go to a better place," but he must have at least wished that Toshi would be one of the many who did. A prayer for Toshi, an individual who was related to him, and the idea that "we are all brothers and sisters of old" are naturally conflicting in some way.

The "I think" in the words "I have never, I think" reflects his wavering mind. The vector toward the absolute truth that everything in this universe is linked and the vector toward the personal relationship with Toshi inevitably come out of alignment.

This misalignment was expressed in another poem just before Toshi's death:

> I and another individual soul try to go everywhere together, perfectly and infinitely. This coalescence is called love.... Now, open your eyes and pull yourself together and follow faithfully the laws of physics and objective phenomena that anyone can see.
>
> ("Koiwai nōjō" [Koiwai Farm])

Here we see the misalignment between his wish to become one with Toshi and his resolution to try to follow the laws of physics. As this misalignment is further amplified, it gradually pushes Kenji toward the latter.

> The timothy grass has become so short,
> blown successively by the wind.
> (They are like blue piano keys pressed down by the wind one after another.)
> Even though the sea is so beautifully blue,
> I am still thinking of Toshi. "Why do you mourn only for your sister?"

So say the faces of distant people and my own inner self.
(*Casual observer! Superficial traveler!*)
                      ("Ohōtsuku banka" [Okhotsk Lament];
                      English in italics is Miyazawa's)

The sea shines blue, the wind sways the timothy grass—this is the great linked world. Toshi has certainly returned to this linked world. Kenji's wish to think of his beloved sister as somehow separate and special has now been placed within this larger world and become quiescent. He thinks that he is simply grieving over grief; that he is nothing but a casual, irresponsible observer or a superficial traveler. He tries to push himself toward the wind, the sea, and the linkage of the world.

His feelings for the individual Toshi do not disappear, however. Despite all his effort, at the very end of the series of his laments, he writes:

> No matter how many times my reason tells me otherwise, my loneliness is not healed....
> It is too deep for that.
> (Loneliness like this is called death.)
> Even if Toshi is smiling quietly
> in a different, radiant world,
> my feelings, warped by sorrow,
> cannot help thinking of her as hiding somewhere.
>   ("Funkawan (Nokutān)" [Volcano Bay (Nocturne)])

Considering, as Kenji did, the linkage of the whole universe as the absolute truth, he tries to go toward it, but at the same time he cannot help thinking of Toshi as hiding somewhere and clings to her as an individual. Warped by sorrow, Kenji is left in loneliness.

From "Beloved Ones" to "Everyone's Happiness"

The issue here is the ultimate destination of *kanashimi* (sorrow) and *sabishisa* (loneliness), or how the existence of the being known as Toshi might be pacified.

> Orderly floating channel buoys,
> the pristine air, dew on shallot leaves,
> the ceaseless sad murmur
> of water flowing nightlong toward the Southern Cross.
> ......
> O Water, please take the unfocused sorrow
> overflowing my bosom
> to the far-off Magellanic Clouds.
> There, fishing lamps are flickering red
> and scorpions creep on thin clouds.
> ... Eternally contriving, eternally grieving, eternally impoverished,
> it flows endless....
> Ah, what a good thing it is
> that we don't know
> where our beloved one has gone in the hereafter.
>
> ("Kairosei" [Dew on Shallot Leaves])

"Dew on Shallot Leaves," written immediately after the laments, is said to contain some of the ideas found in his later novel *Ginga tetsudō no yoru* (*Night on the Galactic Railroad*; also translated as *Milky Way Railroad*). The last three lines read as follows in another version of the poem:

> Ah, real happiness comes to people
> because they don't know
> where their beloved ones have gone in the hereafter.

From the first version to the second Kenji has turned his attention from the greatest happiness for the individual to the greatest happiness for everyone. Subsequently, he threw himself into peasant movements to achieve happiness for all, and in the end he ruined his health.

In any case, it is my impression that "Ah, what a good thing it is / that we don't know / where our beloved one has gone in the hereafter" cannot be regarded as an indication that Kenji had successfully accepted the "unfocused sorrow overflowing my bosom" that had been there since "Wailing Inaudibly." "Dew on Shallot Leaves" was originally written in pencil and then erased, but later deciphered and recovered. Even though it had been once erased, it is also true that it was originally conceived and written in this way. In my *The Philosophy of "Sorrow,"* I tracked Kenji's spirit and wrote that his *kanashimi* had nowhere "to go," though he was trying hard to find an outlet in the greatest happiness for everyone.

In the same book I took up the lyrics of a song translated into

Japanese by Arai Man, called "Sen no kaze ni natte" (Becoming a Thousand Winds). The lyrics begin:

> Do not stand at my grave and weep.
> I am not there. I do not sleep.
> A thousand winds, I have become a thousand winds
> Blowing through the skies.

The tenor of this poem is similar to Kenji's attempt to cease following the individual Toshi and to see her in the timothy grass, the blowing wind, and find the real force of Toshi there. The deceased individual is no longer here and has become the wind, and should not be lamented. I brought this notion into question by citing the thoughts of Yanagita Kunio and Motoori Norinaga, who advocated that a person's death should be mourned heart and soul.

In November 2009, after I finished writing *The Philosophy of "Sorrow,"* I had an opportunity to take part in a convention, The 21st Century Mt. Koya Medical Forum, and talk with Yanagida Kunio. I asked him what he thought of Kenji's *kanashimi* toward Toshi, and how Kenji came to the "conclusion" that it was a good thing that we didn't know where our loved ones had gone after death. We had discussed a related matter at an earlier symposium.

Yanagida, carefully choosing his words, replied that in the last part of *The Little Prince*, the prince, who was going to return to his home star, said, "The star is so small that you cannot tell which it is. But it is better that way. My star will just be one of the stars in the night sky. And you will learn to love watching all the stars in the heavens ... they will all become your friends." Yanagida also added that, sometime after the loss of his son, he came to feel, when he saw young people like his son, that he wanted to do something for them.

Indeed, Kenji's statement "Ah, what a good thing it is / that we don't know / where our beloved one has gone in the hereafter" included the notion that "Ah, real happiness comes to people / because they don't know," and Kenji strove to make his way in that direction.

The question I had been struggling with from the beginning was raised again. At that time I had finished writing the main text of *The Philosophy of "Sorrow,"* so I just added an "Afterword," saying this issue would be dealt with at a later date.

This is the question then: how should we reconcile the loss of a beloved one, the *tomurai* or *itami* of the dead as an individual, with the wish for the happiness (*saiwai*) of other people, not to say of everyone in the whole world?

A Single Spirit and the Pure Love for Everyone

In response to that question, I would like to reconsider my thoughts on the subject thus far. I will cite once again Nishida Kitarō's passage on the loss of his beloved daughter in his introduction to *The History of Japanese Literature*, but this time a little more carefully.

> A dead person never comes back to life, so they tell me to accept it and forget about her. However, for a parent this would be unbearable.... Somehow or other I want to remember her. I want to leave some memorial to her. At the very least, I want to remember her while I am still alive. This is what it means to be a parent.... To remember her from time to time, from occasion to occasion, is the least I can do to alleviate my suffering and to take care of the dead with all my heart. This anguish is truly tormenting, but the parent does not want the pain to go away.... However worthless a person might be, a single spirit cannot be compensated by other things. This absolute value of human life is most painfully felt when we have lost a child.

As we saw earlier, what Nishida says here is that the dead can express absolute worth as individual spirits as long as the living direct their *itami* toward them. This is also the meaning of the sentence excerpted below, "The spiritual life of a human being is not so insignificant." I would like to cite this passage once again to include previous elisions.

> At any rate, I learned numerous lessons from the sad death of my child. Feeling as though a ladleful of cold water had been splashed on my mind, which was busy seeking after worldly interests, I felt a kind of coolness, as if clear, warm autumn sunlight were coming from the back of my mind: I could feel a pure love for all

people. Especially, what moved my mind most deeply was the question: Why does a lovely child, who was talking, singing, and playing up until just now, suddenly disappear, reduced to white bones in an urn? If this is life, life is absurd. A deep meaning must be there. The spiritual life of a human being is not so insignificant.

(Introduction to *The History of Japanese Literature*)

The omitted part was "I felt a kind of coolness, as if clear, warm autumn sunlight were coming from the back of my mind: I could feel a pure love for all people." When we read this part with the rest of the text, we can see that Nishida's phrase "the spiritual life of a human being is not so insignificant" was not confined to the confirmation of the single spirit of his beloved daughter, but also included "clear, warm autumn sunlight" and his feeling of pure love for all people.

Nishida's approach through his own experience and thought, which does not confine the meaning of his daughter's death to her single self, leads to the conclusion expressed in the final sentences of his introduction to *The History of Japanese Literature*:

Last of all, no one is free from various illusions in the face of an event like the death of one's child. One's mind is disturbed by futile self-recrimination, thinking belatedly that I should have done this or I should have done that. However, one has no choice but to accept one's fate, which moves from an inward as well as an outward direction. Behind our faults there seems to be a controlling mysterious power.... When we deeply realize how powerless we are, abandon ourselves and take refuge in some absolute force, self-recrimination will change into penitence. It is as if our mind has unloaded a heavy burden, and we can feel relief and offer an apology to the dead person. We can catch glimpses of such noble beliefs as those that appear in the *Tannishō*—"I am not absolutely certain whether the *nenbutsu* (a prayer to Amida Buddha) may be the cause of my rebirth in the Pure Land or whether that act will send me to hell"—and we can once again come in contact with infinite new life.

The expression "spiritual life" in "the spiritual life of a human being is not so insignificant" is not, of course, different from the "infinite new life" at the end of the preceding paragraph. When Nishida realized the inability of *mizukara* and re-accepted a mysterious power, which he says works behind us all, he could confirm the single spirit of his daughter and could feel pure love for all.

We will recall that Mita's previous question—"What does it mean to really sublimate a dead person?"—produced the following: "This is a thought to light the whole world, filled with worldly things, and at the same time from within." This is similar to Nishida's explanation. After the words "really sublimate a dead person" comes "**the recognition** to shed light, from within, on the flowers produced by the person **who lived**, or the colors of the life of the flowers." Mita continues as follows:

… This is the way Ishimure concretely sublimated each of the deceased of Minamata in her works.

This same approach is also the way to sublimate the living, that is, to awaken the flowers that are already blooming within the body of the living and to provide the vital spark of reality. The perception of "being sublime" is the only way to enliven the living as it is the only way to enliven the dead. Like the brightness of the sun dancing in the hollow caves of the mortal world, this way of thought brightens from within the whole world and its throngs of individual objects.

("Thinking that Sublimates the World")

Next I would like to reconsider how the acts of *shōgon* and *tomurai* of "a single spirit" expands and develops into a feeling of pure love for all people or a way of thinking that "lights a lamp for the whole world."

From the Living to the Dead, and From the Dead to the Living

I would like again to take up Kaneko Daiei's concept of "flower petals fall, but the flower endures." In fact, this idea also contains the above-mentioned expansion and development. This phrase originally appeared in the following text:

Flower petals fall, but the flower endures. The form perishes, but the being endures. Eternity lies in the depths of the present and shines into the future, and permanent presence lies outside of life and death and becomes the light to illuminate life and death. The only way to sense the eternal light is the *nenbutsu* Namu Amidabutsu.

(*Tannishō ryōge* [Understanding the *Tannishō*])

Kaneko often penned the following calligraphy: "'Emptiness is form' equals Namu Amidabutsu." This also confirms "Form is emptiness; emptiness is form." The basic understanding of "flower petals fall, but the flower endures. / The form perishes, but the being endures" is that "flower petals" as a form may fall and perish, but the "flower" that "lies in the depths of the present and shines into the future" is a permanent presence. Paraphrasing the words of Matsubara Taidō, the "eternal light" emerges when we have a sudden insight (*shōken*) and see things, as it were, through two lenses, one to pierce the transient (*shikisokuzekū*) and the other to recognize the true state of emptiness (*kūsokuzeshiki*). This fact is confirmed by chanting the *nenbutsu*.

However, even given this perception, it is a little difficult to understand how the "eternal light" of the flower that endures is considered as becoming the light to illuminate life and death. In other words, the flower that endures, as seen in the previous chapter, should not be considered in terms of mere facticity but rather in the relationship of our acts of *tomurau* and *itamu*. The words "become the light to illuminate life and death" bring the condition, meaning, and directionality of the relationship into question once again.

To put it simply, in the words "becomes the light to illuminate life and death" we have to understand that the dead, as the "flower," become the light to illuminate the world of life and death, or our world of the living. This relational reversal, as we might say, is stated delicately, but this seems to be an important point of Kaneko's argument.

The passage "flower petals fall, but the flower endures" is placed after the following two passages, where one can see the direction of Kaneko's thinking. The immediately preceding passage is as follows:

> On a moonlit night I think of a faraway friend. I become the moonlight and visit this friend. I visit he who is sick, bearing flowers. I become the flowers and express sympathy at his sickbed. When deeply moved, a physical body can still perform acts freely. Further, if we become one with the eternal truth, what can we not do if we have the will? At that time, I will effortlessly become every form and acquire divine power, and every form will effortlessly become me and spread the words of Buddha. (*Understanding the Tannishō*)

Moreover, the following paragraph precedes the one above:

> Ancestors who return by our remembering them will all become buddhas and console us. As a result, we will also become buddhas and emerge in the mind of posterity. We will become soft light, creep through a

window, and visit a room as a cool breeze, without a sound. At that time, we will have no form or name, so we will be able to freely console people without troubling them, and to safely protect them without being noticed. It is heartwarming just to contemplate it.

(*Understanding the Tannishō*)

Both passages are a little difficult to understand, but the important thing is that both are related from the viewpoint of the dead for the living. In other words, I had always thought of "flower petals fall, but the flower endures" and "the form perishes, but the being endures" in terms of *tomurau* and *itamu* of the living for the dead, but here it is considered in terms of the dead reaching out to the living.

According to the doctrine called *gensō-ekō* (returning from the Pure Land to this world in order to succor the living), this means that ancestors return in our remembering them from the Pure Land as buddhas to console us. As buddhas, the dead sometimes become soft light, sometimes cool wind, comforting and protecting the living freely and unhindered.

The notion of free and unhindered light and cool wind will be considered immediately below, but here I would like to confirm that this is taken as coming from the other side, from the side of the dead. Of course, this cannot be seen as being different from the acts of *tomurau* and *itamu* of the living for the dead. It is not that the dead simply come from the Pure Land to console and protect us without any relationship to the actions of the living. Kaneko says on a different occasion:

> Anyone who has been bereaved of his parents or a child, and who prays for them, undoubtedly realizes this. The *nenbutsu* chanted after we have lost a parent will be different from the *nenbutsu* chanted before that event, containing something powerful and rich, though we are praying to the same Buddha. Therefore, if we experience the loss of our father or mother, bereave the departure of Saint Shinran, and pray to Buddha according to *gensō-ekō*, Buddha will be there to help us, to console and support us.
>
> ("Tariki hongan," *Watashi no jinseikan*
> ["Reliance on the Other," My View Of Life])

The *nenbutsu* seems to contain "something powerful and rich, though we are praying to the same Buddha" because the dead return as *gensō-ekō* buddhas after the dead have received *tomurau* and *itamu*. This is the true nature of what Kaneko refers to as the "flower that endures."

It is the same process that Nishida, upon the death of his beloved daughter, engages in—namely, the acts of *tomurau* and *itamu* with a wish "to remember her while I am still alive." He says, "I felt a kind of coolness, as if clear, warm autumn sunlight was coming from the back of my mind: I could feel pure love for everyone," while at the same time perceiving his daughter as one of the dead. The sentence "The spiritual life of a human being is not so insignificant" implies that such a "mysterious force" is in operation.

This is the same situation that Yanagida Kunio, in the *tomu-*

rau and *itamu* of the eternal life of the dead, describes as a wonder taking place; that is, by unceasingly speaking of those possessing eternal life, the living inversely receive the "warm energy of life" (*How to Discover "the Answer to Human Life"*).

Here is another citation from Kaneko's text that delicately narrates the subtlety of the intersection between the living and the dead.

> Then, I remember familiar people who are faraway and acquaintances who have recently passed on. I have no choice but to use the word "remember" here, but this is not really suitable. I feel as if I am meeting the souls of these people within my own somewhat lonely soul. Soul and soul speak with one another, without words. The scope of this feeling expands by turn in every direction, so that I see into the minds of my remote ancestors and listen to the whispering of every living soul.
>
> ("Jinsei no yukue," *Jūnishō*
> ["The Destination of Life," Twelfth Annotation])

Kaneko says that as souls encounter or talk with each other, something that should not be reduced to either remembering or being remembered, the area of this notion expands in every direction, and in turn reaches the point where we listen to the internal whispering of every living thing. This is, once again, "a thought that lights a lamp from within for the whole world and everything in it."

How to Render *Itoshisa*

Thus, in the acts of *tomurau* and *itamu* by the living, the individual contours of the dead are never lost. Tendō Arata writes, "I want to remember the deceased as unique beings who cannot be replaced by any other person. I call this *itamu*" (*The Mourner*). On the other hand, as the dead return from the Pure Land to this world as *gensō-ekō* buddhas, they are mentioned as beings or functions that have "no form or name," and which are said to visit the living as free and unhindered light or wind.

This two-way narration exemplifies the issue of the misalignment mentioned by Miyazawa Kenji in his feelings for Toshi as an individual and his feelings for her as an entity linked to the whole universe. To consider again this issue based on what we have seen so far, the words "Ah, what a good thing it is / that we don't know / where our beloved one (*itoshiku omou mono*) has gone in the hereafter" ("Dew on Shallot Leaves") obviously do not mean that our tender feeling (*itoshisa*) for the deceased herself is gone. By saying it is "a good thing," Kenji tries to place his beloved sister in the linkage and scope of the whole universe.

> Ah, real happiness comes to people because they don't know where their beloved one has gone in the hereafter.

In the alternative version we saw earlier, it seems that Kenji desperately wanted to think that the *itoshisa* toward beloved ones and the fact that "real happiness comes to people" are not contradictory, or at least do not oppose each other. Possibly Kenji had this in mind when he wrote the following well-known passage in *Night on the Galactic Railroad*, where a man explains to the protagonist that he cannot accompany his deceased friend in death:

> But you cannot go with Campanella. And everyone is Campanella. Think of all the people you have ever met, of everyone you have ever shared an apple with or taken a train ride with. So, as you inferred earlier, you should look for the greatest happiness for everyone and make haste to go with them. Only then can you be with Campanella forever.

No matter how much he wants it, he cannot go together with the individual Toshi (Campanella). However, if he looks for the greatest happiness for everyone and goes with them to their ultimate destination, then he can be with Campanella forever.

In Kaneko's commentary on the *Tannishō* (*Understanding the Tannishō*) there is an interesting series of passages on Chapter 4, including his thoughts on "flower petals fall, but the flower endures":

> There is a difference in the mercy of the Holy Path of Buddhism and the Pure Land. The mercy of the Holy Path is expressed through pity, sympathy, and care for all things, but it is rare that one can help others as completely as one desires. Mercy in the Pure Land is to quickly become a buddha by reciting the *nenbutsu*,

and with the great heart of mercy and love to save people as we desire. In this life, however much pity and sympathy we may feel for others, it is impossible to help them as we truly wish. Therefore, our mercy is inconsistent and limited. Only by reciting the *nenbutsu* can absolute mercy, which is true, real, and sincere, be manifested.

In this world, regardless of how "much pity and sympathy we may feel," our desire to succor people is not fulfilled. This passage says we should become a buddha and fulfill our wishes by believing in Amida's vow to save all sentient beings and by practicing the *nenbutsu*.

Kenji's quite altruistic concept of mercy was expressed as "I don't care if my body is consumed by fire one hundred times for everyone's happiness" (*Night on the Galactic Railroad*). Nevertheless, this passage was not considered as rejecting Kenji's desire to go and be with Toshi.

I think this is not so different from what Shinran said in Chapter 5 of the *Tannishō*:

> I, Shinran, have never said the *nenbutsu* out of filial piety. Everything is father and mother, brother and sister, in the worldly process of birth and death. When Buddhahood is attained in the next life, everyone will be saved.... When enlightenment is swiftly attained in the Pure Land, intimately connected people will be saved first through a mysterious power, regardless of

how deeply they are immersed in the karmic agony of
the six realms of being (*rikudō*) and the four modes of
birth (*shishō*).

It seems that Shinran believed that to save everyone and to save the personally connected first do not oppose or exclude one another.

Considering the above from the viewpoint of the *awai* (shifting boundary) between *onozukara* and *mizukara*, our *mizukara* acts of *tomurau* and *itamu* may never be complete, no matter how urgently we try. In this case, not only our *mizukara* power, but also the *onozukara* function that exceeds *mizukara*, is necessary, and our acts will be performed within *onozukara*. This is the mysterious power to which linkage is attempted, as mentioned by Nishida and others, and which Kaneko (and Shinran) regard as a function of Amida Buddha and Kenji as an authentic force. The *nenbutsu* and the practices of Bodhisattvas on their path to Buddhahood can be perceived as acts to link the *awai* between *mizukara* and *onozukara*.

CHAPTER 4

What Is *Shiawase*?

What a joy it is to lead an abundant life!
What a joy!

Zeami

Shiawase

"The greatest happiness for everyone" and "genuine happiness" are ideals that Miyazawa Kenji sought as requirements for the absolute truth of the universe. Indeed, the discussion of happiness has been one of the central themes of ethics throughout the ages.

What is happiness, and what is happiness like? How is it related to our way of perceiving the world and our lives, as well as our way of viewing our relationship with others? What should we do to obtain it, and how might we fail to obtain it?

This is one of the important questions that has been repeatedly asked throughout the spiritual history of the Japanese people. I believe the discussion of how happiness has been perceived in Japan should be brought within the framework of the question of the *awai* between *onozukara* and *mizukara*. In this chapter I will present a holistic discussion of this subject.

As a foundation for this undertaking, I will consider the formation of words signifying happiness, something which I have done before but will do again here more conscientiously.

The formation of each word as such is naturally affected by the multilayered overlapping of the thoughts and feelings of the people living at the time. We can already see the function of *awai* between *onozukara* and *mizukara* in this overlapping, but I think we can particularly see this function in the words *shiawase* (happiness), *medetashi* (auspicious), *iwau* (celebrate), *saiwai* (good fortune), and *sachi* (luck).

We will begin with the word *shiawase* as defined by the *Iwanami Classical Dictionary*.

>
> *Shiawase*
> 1. (verb with lower bigrade conjugation: *shiawasu*)
>   Align to fit closely.
>
>   *Ōku no monodomo sonjite, kyō no kuyō ni shiawasu beki ni arazu* (Since many things have been damaged, they do not fit closely with today's ceremony.)
>   > (*Kohon setsuwashū* [Collection of Old Tales])
>
>   *Sahai wa keikō anbai nari. Ategai shiawasuru nari* (Direction means consideration of the circumstances. It means application and fitting.)
>   > (*Daikeishoshō* [Commentaries on the Book of Great Wisdom])
>
> 2. (noun)
> i. Fortune. Luck. Used in both positive and negative senses.
>   *Shiawase waruku shite, rakudai-shita zo* (I had bad luck and failed the test.)
>   > (*Santaishishō* [Commentaries on a Collection of Chinese Poetry That Includes Three Classic Styles])

> *Kyō wa shiawase yoku haberite!* (Today we have good fortune!)
>
> ("Tsuru no okina," *Otogi zōshi*
> ["An Old Crane Man," A Fairy Tale Book])

ii. Especially: good luck.

> *Sonata wa tenkaichi no shiawase na hito ja* (You are the happiest person under heaven.)
>
> ("Busshi," *Tenribon kyōgen rikugi* ["A Sculptor of Buddhist Images," Kyōgen Scripts in the Tenri Library])

The noun *shiawase* derives from the verb *shiawasu*. Its original meaning is to align so as to closely fit by *mizukara* (voluntary) effort. We *shiawasu* because we encounter unexpected and unpredictable situations, in response to which we need to "make alignments," take circumstances into consideration (*keikō anbai*), and make preparations for each need (*ategau*).

However, when the verb *shiawasu* is nominalized into *shiawase*, it takes on the additional meaning of "fortune" or "luck." Generally, when words are nominalized and conceptualized, a certain inherent element or inclination is amplified and becomes established. I think that this is the case here.

Here we can see the attitude that *shiawase* is brought about not by *mizukara* effort but is greatly dependent on functions beyond it. Initially it was used in both positive and negative senses, as in *shiawase waruku shite* (had bad luck) and *shiawase yoku* (have good fortune), but later *shiawase* was confined to the meaning of *yoki shiawase* (good fortune). As early as the late Middle Ages it is said to have taken on this meaning.

In our consideration of the transition of meanings in the word *shiawase*, we can introduce the perspective of the *awai* between *onozukara* and *mizukara*. *Shiawase* describes a situation where something is accomplished or made possible. As we have seen earlier, we sometimes refer to resultant outcomes as having "emerged" or "turned out" (*idekita*) a certain way even when they are the result of a *mizukara* effort. Something similar can be seen in *shiawase*, where everything in this world exists in the *awai* between *mizukara* effort and *onozukara* function.

In other words, while the Japanese view of *shiawase* is based on our *mizukara* efforts to fit (*shiawasu*) and calculate (*hakaru*), it contains an *awai* boundary between such efforts and the unforeseeable and incalculable *onozukara* (the Heavens, gods or Buddha)—that is, something the self is unable to control.

Medetashi

Every year I receive a New Year's greeting card from a Chinese friend containing the phrase *banji nyoi* (may everything go as you wish). In this felicitous wish for *shiawase* during the coming year, there seems to be something very different from the Japanese way of thinking.

To the Japanese mind, "happiness" arises in the *awai* boundary as part of the interplay between the involuntary *onozukara* and the voluntary *mizukara*. The concept of *banji nyoi* is somewhat different from this. In the Chinese way of thinking, I cannot help but feel they want things to go strictly according to their likes and dislikes.

At the beginning of a New Year, it is the Japanese custom to greet one another with the words *Omedetō gozaimasu* (roughly, "Congratulations"). This is quite different from *banji nyoi*, but what does *omedetō* or *medetai* (in its dictionary form) mean? First of all, let us take a closer look at *medetai* and its older form *medetashi*.

In the *Iwanami Classical Dictionary*, *medetashi* is explained as follows:

Medetashi
Abbreviation of *mede* (love) *itashi* (extremely).
1. Perfectly wonderful. Nothing but admiration.
2. Fine and good. Celebratory.
3. Good-natured and easily deceived. A simpleton. Thickheaded.

As we see from this dictionary entry, *medetashi* is a variation of *medeitashi*, a word composed of *mede* from *mederu* (to love) and *itashi* (extremely), meaning: 1) "Perfectly wonderful" and 2) "Fine and good. Celebratory."

The *Shogakukan Nihon kokugo daijiten* (Shogakukan Complete Japanese Language Dictionary) explains that, as a polite phrase after the early modern period, the conjunctive form of *omedetai* (with the honorific prefix *o*)—*omedetaku*—was changed into *omedetō*, which began to be used to precede such polite verbs as *zonjimasu* and *gozaimasu*.

Anything to be celebrated, such as success in an examination or finding employment, is generally considered *medetai*. The most typical cases characterized as *medetai* are the four major ceremonies of life (*kankonsōsai*), with the exception of *sō* (funerals). *Kan* refers to rites of passage such as the coming of age ceremony, *kon* to marriage, and *sai* to yearly events.

The content of *medetai* changes a little whether in reference to rites of passage, marriage or yearly events. The New Year is the occasion when the greeting *omedetō* is most frequently exchanged. It is used to celebrate the fact that everyone has been able to start the year anew, as in the expression *Shinnen, akemashite omedetō gozaimasu* (It is good fortune to greet the New Year). Here "everyone" basically takes the family as a single unit; consequently, this greeting is not offered to those who have lost a family member in the previous year.

That is, the word *omedetō* in the New Year's greeting expresses gratitude, celebration, and a sanguine wish for the past, present, and future—that is, gratitude that all the family members were able to live through the previous year safely, celebration that all are able to commence the New Year, and a wish that everyone will safely live through the coming year.

The same thinking applies to other occasions of rites of passage, marriage or yearly events. When we say *omedetō* at a coming of age ceremony, we use it to celebrate the very fact that the person has reached adulthood but also to express the wish that he or she will flourish in the future as a member of society.

This is also true of marriage. With the words *omedetō gozaimasu*, people express their gratitude and celebration of the fact that it has turned out that the couple will marry, amid circumstances beyond *mizukara* control, including the initial encounter with a marriage partner, various intervening events, and other people's help, accompanied by a prayer and wish that their married life will continue happily (*shiawase ni*) into the future.

Iwau

The word *iwau* (to celebrate) now seems to be limited to certain felicitous events, but originally it was freely used in various types of prayers. This was due to the fact that the ceremonies of rites of passage, marriage and yearly events took place as Shinto or Buddhist rites.

The *Iwanami Classical Dictionary* explains *iwau* as follows:

> *Iwau*
> Originally meant to utter auspicious words and perform propitious acts and incantations to promote felicity, safety, or happiness.
> 1. Perform good deeds to secure future happiness and safety. Avoid doing what is deemed bad.
> 2. While incanting, perform acts miming the desired *shiawase*.
> 3. Utter incantatory words seeking felicity and perform divine rituals.
> 4. Wish for future happiness and utter auspicious phrases.
> 5. Perform a festival for the gods.
> 6. Enshrine as a god.

Basically, *iwau* is used not for the celebration of *medetai* situations that have already taken place, but rather as a prayer or incantation for future felicity, safety, and happiness contingent on the situation.

What we can do to secure future happiness is, first of all, to conduct ourselves morally in our daily lives with *mizukara* effort and likewise to perform good deeds, as well as to avoid doing what is deemed bad. Traditionally, this has been considered part of our *iwau* conduct, but clearly this is not enough. As in the meanings #2 to #4, it is necessary to perform divine rituals such as performing acts that mime the desired *shiawase* while uttering incantatory words and auspicious phrases. More precisely, the fundamental origin of *iwau* was, as is seen in meanings #5 and #6, to fete or enshrine a god.

This is connected with the Japanese original view of *onozukara* and its contingent, unexpected and "immeasurable" function, exceeding all imagination and beyond our ability to calculate. It has the ambivalent character of allowing us to live and nourishing us as well as harming and destroying us. Later I will look at this point in greater detail.

We can easily imagine that, for the ancient Japanese, *onozukara* phenomena, which brought disasters such as famine, plague, flood, and earthquake, were sources of fear and trembling. To cope with this, they needed to identify what caused the phenomena, give it a name, and make offerings to, and enshrine, the malevolent god. They prayed for safety and health in doing so, and this is what *iwau* meant. That is, *iwau* was inseparable from the acts of *matsuru* (enshrining) and *inoru* (praying).

The acts referred to in meanings #1 to #4 of *iwau* are to utter auspicious phrases and incantatory words, perform miming and propitious acts and incantations in the present for future happiness and safety. In this sense, *iwau* is the act of *yoshuku*, which means "*iwau* in advance." However, this is not an act of calculation (*hakaru*) as discussed earlier, but an act of aligning to fit closely (*shiawasu*) with something unable to be subjected to calculation.

Omoshiroshi

The concept of *yoshuku* also underlies the traditional performing art of Noh. By *iwau* in advance, Noh intended to bestow *medetasa* (auspiciousness; noun form of *medetai*) on the spectators.

Zeami thought of Noh, or *sarugaku*, as a form of entertainment that was also a prayer for peace over the land, saying, "When a *sarugaku* is performed, the country becomes peaceful and the people untroubled and enjoy longevity" (*Fūshikaden* [Transmission of the Flower through the Forms]).

> Basically, the performing arts are a way to soothe people's minds and, by emotionally moving both higher and lower classes, to bring them happiness and proffer a prayer for their longevity.
>
> (*Transmission of the Flower through the Forms*)

While characterizing Noh in this way, Zeami also explains its origins as follows:

Sarugaku is said to have existed since the age of the gods. When Amaterasu Ōmikami secluded herself in a cave, the world became pitch dark. All the gods and goddesses gathered at the cave on Mt. Ama no Kaguyama and performed a play to sacred *kagura* music to honor her.... Amaterasu opened the door to the cave a little. The earth became bright again. The faces of the gods also shone white. The play performed at that time is said to have been the beginning of *sarugaku*.

(*Transmission of the Flower through the Forms*)

According to Zeami, not only was the sacred *kagura* music that the gods played and danced the origin of Noh, it was also the origin of the word *omoshiroshi* ("faces [shining] white"). In the Noh of Zeami the word *omoshiroshi* became an important key concept. Zeami's understanding of *omoshiroshi* will be discussed later; here we will look at the formation of the word *omoshiroshi* (modern *omoshiroi*) itself.

Omoshiroshi

Omo means surface side, front side, or immediately facing side. *Shiroshi* means white.

Omoshiroshi means to see something that is brilliant or a scene that is dazzling and to have one's eyes suddenly opened. It also means to be in a pleasant mood. This meaning spread to indicate the pleasure obtained from music and convivial social gatherings and gradually to the intellectual satisfaction derived

from literature and the decorative arts.
1) (When the surrounding scenery and natural features are bright and cheerful), one is put in a pleasant mood.
2) (When the heart is responsive), there is a feeling of genuine pleasure.
3) One feels attracted. One feels intrigued.

(Iwanami Classical Dictionary)

From the above we can see that *omoshiroshi* originally meant that the landscape or scene in front of one or immediately facing one appeared white. Fields and mountains stretching out in front of our eyes are *omoshiroshi*; the moon shining white in the sky is *omoshiroshi*. In the 10th-century *Taketori monogatari* (Tale of the Bamboo Cutter), there is the line *Tsuki no omoshirō idetaru o mite…*, ("Seeing the moon rise white in the sky…"), where *omoshirō*—a variant of *omoshiroshi*—carries the word's original meaning and describes the physical appearance of the moon.

According to *Nihongo no nenrin* (Growth Rings of the Japanese Language) by Ōno Susumu (1919–2008), *omoshiroshi* was frequently used in the Nara and Heian periods (8th through 12th centuries) to describe an expansive, luminous landscape or scene, but later the word came to refer to the exhilaration felt by those who saw such scenes and found them delightful, amusing, or intriguing.

There is an important implication in the fact that *omoshiroshi* moved away from its original meaning of a landscape or scenery being *omoshiroshi* and came to signify that our hearts open up and feel delight in seeing them. This is because the process shows that what is *omoshiroshi* cannot be realized by operating our *mizukara* mind alone, but the word is used where there is something bright and shining outside of us and we feel delighted and vibrant within when we see it.

To return to Zeami's theory of the origin of Noh, you will recall that he recounted the legend of Amaterasu emerging from a cave and that the faces of the gods shone brightly. This is the origin of the word *omoshiroshi*, he stated. He also added that *kagura* was offered to entice Amaterasu out of the cave, and that this was the origin of Noh.

The bright shining light of Amaterasu is the symbol of the greatness that works at the root of every living thing in this world. Since Noh is the performing art that produces such a function, it is crucially important to know whether it is *omoshiroshi* or not.

> What you see as *omoshiroshi* should be considered the flower of Noh.
>
> (*Transmission of the Flower through the Forms*)

The "flower" (*hana*) of Noh is the emotional experience aroused in the audience; that is, according to Zeami, what excites *omoshiroshi* and pleasure is none other than the flower. In his treatises on Noh he examines in great detail the artifices and techniques (*kufū*) of how this is done.

These *kufū* concern how to do intriguing mimicry of old men, mad men, or devils; how to adapt to the mood of the audience of the day; how to calculate the distance between the actor and the audience or to be in accordance with the rhythm of the moment; and how to move your mind fully while moving your body moderately. There is also the matter of concentrating on linking all these skills, as well as improving your current skills by recalling how inept you were as a beginner. Finally, there is, "If it is hidden, it is the flower. If it is not hidden, it is not the flower."

However, *omoshiroshi* is anything but a makeshift measure to appeal to an audience. Its origin relates to the efflux of deep emotions when we encounter the great function that works at the root of this world, as once manifested in the shining faces of the gods who gazed upon the emerging Amaterasu. *Kufū* is a *mizukara* effort to fit elements together (*shiawasu*) in order to express and promote this primeval emotion.

Many Noh themes are bitter and tragic, but they embrace an unwavering conviction that whatever the difficulty might be, its expression lies, ultimately, within the grand function of *omoshiroshi*.

I would like to give an example. In the play entitled *Eguchi*, Zeami depicts the ghost of a harlot as she narrates, deplores, and dances her bitter, piteous, and ungovernable emotions. Finally, with a contortion of her body, she expresses herself as follows:

> Alas, it is all meaningless.
> This world is, after all, a temporary shelter, nothing but a transient abode.
> I enjoin people to pay it no heed.
> All that went before is now gone.

Following this passage, the ghost ascends into the clouds as Fugen Bodhisattva: "She returns to heaven, manifesting herself as Fugen."

Zeami describes this scene with the understanding that the ascension of Fugen is not realized through the elimination of endless worldly desires but, rather, is a vivid concentration and crystallization of them. This description seems abrupt, as was seen in *Obasute*, but we can conclude that Zeami is having the ghost express her feeling of "Alas, it is all meaningless" by depicting a certain affirmative phase that works in conjunction with this feeling.

We can read this in the phrase *omoshiro ya* cried out at the climax of this piece, which comes immediately before the passage starting with "Alas, it is all meaningless":

> ... I have to escape *aware*, the sensitivity to transient things.
> I know this full well,
> but I am often driven by lust and greed....
> My mind wavers over whatever I see and hear.
> *Omoshiro ya.*

The issue here is how we should interpret *omoshiro ya*. It follows the phrase "I know this full well," as well as the reference to the endlessly wavering mind, producing the lament "Alas, it is all meaningless." The eyes of Zeami are fully fixed on the endlessly "wavering mind" and the notion that "Alas, it is hopeless," without which the world would not be *omoshiroshi*. The ghost cries out *omoshiro ya* based on the existence of such a wavering mind.

We need to understand the above in the context of Zeami's life, for at the advanced age of seventy-two he was banished to the island of Sado. Despite this most grievous event, he could still write:

> The mountains are *onozukara* high, the sea *onozukara* deep. I devote myself to describing the spirits of the mountains and clouds, the sea and moon. How *omoshiro ya* is the Sado Sea! My eyes are filled with nothing but the green mountains of the world. When I ask the name of the island, they say "Sado"—the Golden Island—a place wonderful beyond description.
> (*Kintōsho* [Book of the Golden Island])

Here there is an underlying recognition and affirmation that, no matter how much we grieve or suffer, the expression of that grief or suffering leads to the universal *onozukara* function of *omoshiro ya*, much as it does with the singing of birds or the chirping of insects.

In a Noh performance, the *medetai* celebratory introduction is given first (occasionally last) based on this recognition. This confirms the overarching idea that the *medetai* and *omoshiroi* functions lie at the base of the world. Noh is itself an act of *awai* or *shiawasu* (fitting together) to draw forth these functions with our *mizukara* effort.

Sakiwau and *Saiwai*

The grand *onozukara* function that shines on us as *omoshiroshi* is expressed as a function of *sakiwau*. The word *sakiwau* derives from *saiwai* (good fortune). *Sakiwau* is defined as follows:

> Sakiwau
> *Sakiwau* is a cognate of *saki* (bloom), *sakae* (prosper), and *sakari* (peak). It means to unfold outward as inward forces of growth reach a peak. The *wai* in the noun form (*sakiwai*) is also seen in *nigiwai* (bustling crowd). It refers to lively, vigorous activity.
>
> (*Iwanami Classical Dictionary*)

From the meaning of burgeoning growth and vitality evolved the meaning of meeting with good luck or prospering. For instance, the following example is given in Iwanami's dictionary: *Kotodama no sakiwau kuni*. This means a country where words are vigorously exchanged or a prosperous country.

Thus we can see that *sakiwau* has the favorable connotations of growth and vitality. *Saiwai* is the euphonic transformation of *sakiwai*, the conjunctive form of the verb *sakiwau*. Of these, *saiwai* is now the most frequently used. By way of clarification, here is the definition given in the *Shogakukan Complete Japanese Language Dictionary*:

> Saiwai
> A condition one finds quite favorable and fortunate

and that can be considered to be provided by others, such as the gods or the Buddha. To have good luck. To meet with an auspicious event. To experience good fortune. Or the state of being fortunate. Well-being. Happiness.

The dictionary provides the following example from the circa 9th-century *Ise monogatari* (The Tale of Ise): *Ame no furinu beki toki ni namu miwazuraihaberu. Mi saiwai araba, kono ame wa furaji* (As it is about to rain, I distress myself while gazing at the sky. But if I am blessed with good luck, it will not rain).

Whether it will rain or not is beyond our *mizukara* efforts. It is unpredictable. In this case it would be considered fortunate (*saiwai*) if it did not rain. In the context the functions of outside forces like gods and the Buddha are a principal concern. *Saiwai* is a noun, but it can also be used as an adverb, as in *Saiwai, ame ga furanakatta* (Fortunately, it did not rain). Since ancient times *saiwai* has been frequently used to mean "fortunately" or "opportunely."

The kanji used to write *saiwai* (幸) is shared with the word *sachi* (luck). Here I will quote the *Iwanami Classical Dictionary* concerning *sachi* in its supplementary note to *saiwai*:

> Although *saiwai* also means "happiness," its origin is found in the flourishing of plants that brings happiness to human beings, whereas *sachi* originally referred to an abundance of fish and game bringing similar happiness.

It also states that *sachi* has the same origin as the Korean word *sal* (arrow), meaning 1) an instrument for hunting or fishing, such as a bow and arrow or a fishhook; 2) the ability to harvest game in hunting and fishing; and 3) the extended meaning of happiness.

While the fixed phrases *sachi ōkare* (I wish you much happiness), *umi no sachi* (fruit of the sea), and *yama no sachi* (fruit of the mountains) are still alive today, in general *saiwai* and *sachi* do not seem to be consciously differentiated. In any event, the vigorous vitality at work in the world, be it flourishing plants or abundant game, was referred to as *saiwai* or *sachi*, which were considered the basic requirements for happiness.

Musubi

The *Kojiki*, the 8th-century collection of Japanese myths, describes in story form how Japan achieved stability and prosperity as a nation. At the core of this narrative are the potential for growth and the life force underpinning the world.

As we saw earlier, the *Kojiki* begins with the following statement, *Ame tsuchi no hajime no toki* (When Heaven and Earth began), and continues:

> The names of the gods that came into being in the Plain of High Heaven when Heaven and Earth began were Ame no Minaka-nushi (the god ruling the center of Heaven), next Takami Musubi (the god creating the High Heaven), and next Kami Musubi (the god creating

the gods).... When the Earth was in its infancy, like floating oil drifting around medusa-like, gods sprouted up like reed shoots, who were... And next... And next... And then, Izanagi no Kami, and then his sister Izanami no Kami. *(Kojiki)*

In these opening lines to the *Kojiki*, Maruyama Masao has uncovered what he calls a primordial layer of historical meaning inherent to the Japanese people, describing it as a continuous emergence of successive phenomena. In contrast to the logic of "making" or "creating" often seen in the myths of the rest of the world, the Japanese myth, with its underlying intransitive logic of "coming into being" or "emerging," is characterized by successive materialization in accordance with the momentum inherent in the event itself. This momentum describes a situation where the world is launched into being at the beginning of time and then infinitely develops and unfolds on its own. The operative image is the sprouting of reed shoots, overlapped with images of the *onozukara* growth and proliferation of living things.

The basic image is well represented in the word *musubi* or its older form *musuhi* (creation) as it appears in Taka Mi Musubi no Kami (High Musubi God) and Kami Musubi no Kami (Sacred Musubi God), who are the first gods that caused the world to emerge. Nowadays we do not use the word *musubi* in this sense very often, but for ancient Japanese it signified the utmost primordial function. The *Iwanami Classical Dictionary* provides the following definition:

Musubi
Musu is also seen in *musuko* (son) and *musume* (daughter). It means to increase and proliferate like grass or moss. *Bi* is a cognate for *hi* (sun). In primitive thought *musubi* was a spiritual force that was identified with the supernatural power of the sun. It was a mysterious power that allowed the creation and proliferation of all living things.

As we can see in the *Kojiki*, the primitive notion of spiritual power is identified with the force of the sun and narrated in the story of Taka Mi Musubi no Kami, Kami Musubi no Kami, Izanami no Mikoto and Izanagi no Mikoto, as well as Amaterasu Ōmikami and Susanoo no Mikoto.

Earlier we saw that, in the ceremony of advanced celebration (*yoshuku*), Zeami prayed for a peaceful world in which the people achieved tranquility and enjoyed longevity by employing the power of regeneration and revitalization through Amaterasu Ōmikami. Today we still celebrate this power when we sing the Japanese national anthem: *Kimigayo wa chiyo ni yachiyo ni sazare ishi no iwa to narite koke no musu made* (Thousands of years of happy reign be thine; / rule on, my lord, until what are pebbles now / by ages united to mighty rocks shall grow / whose venerable sides the moss doth line). (Translation by Basil Hall Chamberlain)

The *Iwanami Classical Dictionary* explains that "although [*musubi* as a spiritual force] was later interpreted in connection with *musubi* meaning "tying," the two words are not originally related in terms of meaning, consonant voice, or accent." However, in light of the dictionary's note that *musubi* ("tying") "means to firmly interlock both ends of a rope or the fingers of the hands so that they do not separate from each other," and further that the meaning of "tying pine twigs or grass ends with each other as an incantation for longevity or bountiful happiness," we may see a connection in that the two meanings of *musubi* both refer to an act of *iwau*.

We have already seen that Sagara Tōru, acknowledging a mysterious spiritual power that brings everything into being as living things, explained the *tōtosa* of the *inochi* (life) of all living things as a natural occurrence. The following is a complement to the discussion in Chapter 2, "What Is the Meaning of *Tōtoi?*" *Tōtoshi*, originally a classical Japanese word, is explained as follows:

> *Tafutoshi* [an older spelling of *tōtoshi*]
> *Ta* is a prefix [meaning "many"]. *Futoshi* means "magnitude." Therefore, *tafutoshi* represents a feeling that regards natural phenomena as vigorous and magnificent or refers to a highly esteemed person who is regarded with awe. Later it came to mean "thankful."
> 1) Magnificent. Divine and vigorous. 2) Worthy of awe or respect. 3) Highly ranked. Respectable. 4) Thankful. Grateful.   (*Iwanami Classical Dictionary*)

That natural phenomena are vigorous and magnificent is also a condition of *sakiwau* (to prosper). This relates to the explanation that the original meaning of the word *inochi* is the momentum of breath, and that "the ancients seem to have regarded the fundamental power of living as a function of this invisible momentum." *Inochi* is *tōtoi* because it "occurs naturally and lives here" with the invisible, fundamental power of life. In Chapter 2, we considered this as the mysteriousness of *ichigū*.

Life and Death

As I mentioned earlier, the *onozukara* function is not necessarily a positive force such as the power to grow or flourish. Ancient Japanese longed for the emergence and promotion of positive functions because when negative power manifested itself, it brought contingent or unexpected disaster or death. In the *Kojiki*, finding ways in which people could seal off such negative power is repeatedly stated as an important goal.

In other words, *onozukara* originally functions both positively and negatively for us Japanese, and in the *Kojiki* the ambiguity of *onozukara* is vividly described with a focus on death.

After giving birth to countries and gods, and finally as a consequence of birthing a fire god, the goddess Izanami herself dies. This is recounted in the following myth of the lower world, Yominokuni.

In death Izanami descends to Yominokuni, and her brother and spouse, Izanagi, follows her there to plead with her to return to the upper world. Izanami strictly tells him to wait while she consults with the god of the lower world, and not to gaze upon her in the meanwhile. However, Izanagi cannot wait and turns his eyes on Izanami. Her body is rife with maggots; thunder rumbles far and wide. Izanagi grows frightened and runs away, with Izanami in pursuit. At last Izanagi reaches the border between the lower world and the mortal world, and blocks off the entrance with a huge rock. There they exchange words:

> Izanami no Mikoto says, "My dear beloved, if you do this, I will kill 1,000 people in your country every day." Izanagi no Mikoto replies, "My dear beloved, if you do so, I will construct 1,500 birthing houses every day." Thus 1,000 people die every day, and 1,500 people are born. *(Kojiki)*

Further, the *Kojiki* says, "The posthumous name Yomotsu Ōkami was given to Izanami no Mikoto." That is, Izanami, the great mother goddess who brought about the birth of the country and all the gods, also became the great god of the underworld who causes death.

What is being conveyed through the myth of Izanagi and Izanami is that the function that gives life can also be the function that brings death. What is more important is that, comparing the functions controlling life and death, the function of life outnumbers that of death by 1,500 to 1,000. Each individual has to die, but as a whole the function of life is predominant, and we are called upon to promote that function.

Onozukara functions may be positive on the whole, but on an individual level they can work negatively. How we cope with the two-edged *onozukara* is fundamental to our *shiawase*.

As an example, I would like to examine the thought of the

18th-century Japanese classical scholar Motoori Norinaga. In *Naobi no mitama* (The Way of the Gods), Norinaga says, "We can do nothing about the rampaging spirit of Magatsubi no Kami. How sad!" Magatsubi no Kami is the god of disorder and disaster. All the bad things that happen in this world are due to the raging spirit of this god. Therefore, it cannot be helped and is very sad (*kanashii*).

While Norinaga's means of expression may seem to be cloaked in mystical phraseology, in modern terms he is simply saying that it is a matter of bad luck. There are events we cannot explain in any way, such as when someone who had done nothing wrong is walking in a crosswalk and a truck comes along and hits and kills him, or when someone has cancer even though he has taken great care about his health. Norinaga attributes such bad luck to the raging spirit of Magatsubi no Kami. But when he singles out Magatsubi as the source of such misfortune, a certain response or reaction is required from us.

In the above, "it cannot be helped" simply means that there is nothing we can do about it or it is beyond our control. We have no choice but to accept the situation and say how sad it is. This is true of traffic accidents as well as of disease, but what we know for certain is that we will all eventually die, which is the ultimate inevitability.

In *Suzunoya tōmonroku* (Dialogue at Suzunoya), Norinaga responds to a question about how we can obtain peace of mind in the face of death by saying that inquiry into the afterworld is nothing more than pretentious speculation. This is something we cannot know; what we do know is that death is "sad."

He develops a theory of "peace of mind without peace of mind." He writes that Confucianism and Buddhism attempt to create peace of mind by logical argument concerning the unknowable, and that they are mistaken when they tell us not to lament over extremely sad events. We do not need that kind of peace of mind in the face of death, he argues. We can simply feel sad, and in the grieving mind arises another kind of peace of mind.

For Norinaga, the act of grieving generally means to follow the functions that make this world what it is. "All worldly events are divine works. This is the foremost peace of mind" (*Dialogue at Suzunoya*). Worldly things are all divine works, and by accepting them through grieving, peace of mind comes about.

This also means that we must submit to *onozukara*, which works beyond our vacillating minds. Norinaga often uses the word *onozukara* and employs the phrase *shizen no Shintō* (natural Shinto). He also thinks that the expression of "sadness" in *waka* poetry, or the relief of mind from hearing the poems read, are all functions of *onozukara* or *shizen no tae* (mysteries of nature). "Worldly things are all divine works" can be seen as an extension of this line of thought.

According to Norinaga, while we are basically controlled by such functions as life and death, we cannot comprehend the whole picture. We are all a part of the incomprehensible function of the mystery of nature.

The idea that incomprehensible and mysterious functions are at work in this world is akin to the thought of Shinran. Shinran accepted these functions as being those of Amida Buddha. Although they are mysterious to us ordinary human beings, their aim is thought to be our salvation. Shinran, in later life, said that Amida was "a means of enlightening us about nature and *onozukara*" (*Mattōshō* [Last Letters of Shinran]).

However, Norinaga and Shinran do not mean that *mizukara* should thoughtlessly follow the functions of *onozukara*. Norinaga says in the passage about "peace of mind without peace of mind" that we should follow *onozukara* "with every means at our disposal" (*Dialogue at Suzunoya*). To properly grieve or feel sad (*kanashimu*) means to completely accept the limitations and impotence of *mizukara*. It is an awareness of the fact that we "can do nothing" or "it cannot be helped" (*semu sube nashi*) mentioned above. For Shinran, it is the awareness that we are just ordinary human beings with limited power. Only with such an awareness can we sense the gods and *onozukara* as functions transcending *mizukara*.

Mujō and *Onozukara*

The above discussion leads again to the question of how to interpret *mujōkan*. Generally, *mujōkan* is taken to connote the negative sentiments of *kurushi* (agony), *hakanashi* (fleetingness), or *kanashi* (sorrow). However, these negative sentiments are not sensed or used solely in their negative or passive forms. This is because as *mujō-aware* beings we accept *onozukara* as affirmative and positive when we recognize *mizukara* as a transient, one-time experience in which the self lives and dies. As we have already seen, the poet Ōtomo no Yakamochi, while fully aware of *mujōkan* in his "Lament for the Transient World," also sensed the grand functions of heaven, earth, and nature. The playwright and critic Yamazaki Masakazu (b. 1934) describes this subtlety as follows:

> When we see fireworks on a summer evening exploding and then disappearing, it is true that there is a vague pathos. The Japanese people have long been attracted to *hakanasa* (the fleetingness of life) and indulged themselves in the transience of worldly things. This is certainly true, but it is also true that the same Japanese people did not, curiously enough, abandon themselves to extreme nihilism. While bemoaning the *mujō* of life, our ancestors found that nature was fairly stable. This is undoubtedly due to their ability to detect the smallest momentary change in the order of things, much like the introduction, exposition, and rapid finale of a theatrical performance.
> (*Konton kara no hyōgen* [Expression Out of Chaos])

From this we can see that in its perception of *mujōkan* and *hakanasa*, Japanese sensibility involves a certain sensitivity to order. While bemoaning the *mujō* of life, our ancestors found nature to be fairly stable.

Speaking more generally, the philosopher Isobe Tadamasa (1909–95) has the following to say about the Japanese people's acceptance of the overlapping of the rhythm of *mujō* with the rhythm of stable nature:

> At some time or other, the Japanese people acquired a certain "knack" for surrendering themselves to the flow of what might be called the living rhythm of nature, which includes mankind. This resignation is based on *mujōkan*, which also encompasses one's own strength and will. They are all constituent elements of this grand rhythm—emerging and disappearing, living and dying. ("*Mujō" no kōzō* [The Structure of "*Mujō*"])

Mujōkan is not felt independently as such. When perceived together with the great rhythm of the life of nature, *mujōkan* becomes resignation with one's own power and will, accepting emergence and ruin, life and death as being elements of this great rhythm. There is the Japanese word *akirame* (諦め; resignation) and its homophone 明らめ (clarification), but they are not necessarily the same as *satya*, the Buddhist notion of non-self (諦, *tai*, in Japanese). Japanese resignation preserves the idea of the self who accepts *semu sube nashi* and is *hakanashi* or *kanashi*. The point of this sensitivity is the placement of the self in the flow of this great rhythm while preserving its ability to sense the *mujōkan* of things.

Isobe's notion of "the constituent elements of this grand rhythm" leads to Shiga's "a drop of water in the grandly flowing Nile" that we saw earlier, and further, to the traditional thought of *ichigū* (a special "corner" of the universe). Even though our *mizukara* existence and acts are relative and limited as constituent elements and "corners," they are at the same time part of the grand *onozukara* and therefore absolute and infinite in themselves.

In the passage quoted above, Yamazaki Masakazu attributes to the Japanese people a sensitivity to the stability of nature within *mujōkan* as well as a sense of order that detects the smallest instantaneous change in the arrangement of things, much like the introduction, exposition, and rapid finale of a theatrical performance. This is based on the following idea of Zeami's:

> Looking carefully at Noh, we see that everything in the world, right or wrong, large or small, with or without life, is composed of an introduction, expository, and finale. Even the birds and insects sing accordingly. This is the attainment of a stage beyond social position and the mortal mind. Some are attuned to sound; some are capable of deep feeling. Without this attainment, we would not find things *omoshiroshi* or feel *aware*.
>
> (*Shūgyokutokka* [Gathering Gems and Gaining Flowers])

We have discussed *omoshiroshi* earlier, but here Zeami is saying that *omoshiroshi* and *aware* come when one perceives the rhythm of introduction, exposition, and finale, that is, the grand *onozukara*, and is in synchrony with that rhythm. Furthermore, this is not different from birds and insects singing in accordance with their nature and attaining a certain kind of completion or Buddhahood.

As we saw in the Noh plays *Obasute* and *Eguchi*, which describe the fulfillment and attainment of each of those who suffer and grieve, it doesn't mean that the *mizukara* of each is eliminated by *onozukara*. While each lives his life and dies, each still tries to achieve fulfillment via the *onozukara* rhythm.

In other words, *mizukara* is *mizukara* in every aspect, and at the same time strives to "attain" *onozukara*. As Zeami says, "attainment" (*jōju*) means "to happen to turn out" (*naritsuku*), which in turn means "to settle down at ease" (*rakkyo*) (*Gathering Gems and Gaining Flowers*). Notably, *jōju* and *rakkyo* take place in the *awai* between *onozukara* and *mizukara*.

The Many Meanings of *Sumu*

The current of the flowing river never ceases, and it never changes, with the bubbles on the surface continually gathering, then vanishing, forever clear.

This is a passage from Zeami's celebratory Noh play *Yōrō* (Nurturing the Aged). It is a slight variation on the famous opening lines of Kamo no Chōmei's 13th-century *Hōjōki* (An Account of My Hut). In *An Account of My Hut*, the sentence ends with "never staying long," but Zeami changed this to "forever clear."

In the *mujō* expressed in "never staying long," Zeami discovered something that led him to change it to "forever clear." Water is clear because it is perpetually in motion. In *Nurturing the Aged*, this sentence comes after the following celebratory remarks:

The reign of our lord is indeed clear as a jewel, so that even we of the lower classes can lead an abundant life. What a joy it is to live an abundant life! What a joy!

In this passage the word *sumu* appears twice, one meaning "clear" and the other meaning "to live or reside." Since the word is an important term in Zeami's work, we will focus on it in the discussion below.

In classic Japanese, *sumu* has basically three meanings: clear (澄む or 清む), finish (済む), and reside (住む).

First, the original meaning of 澄む (clear) and 済む (finish) is explained as follows:

> Floating objects sink and come to rest all together; gases and liquids turn transparent.
> *(Iwanami Classical Dictionary)*

Let us look at the examples cited in this dictionary employing 澄む. *Hakatagawa chitose o machite sumeru kawa kamo* means that the muddy river water became clear after 1,000 years (*Shoku Nihongi kayō* [Songs and Poems from the Chronicles of Japan, Sequel]). *Kiyoku sumeru tsuki ni* and *Mono no ne sumu beki yo no sama* describe situations in which light and sounds become free of dullness and are lambent (*The Tale of Genji*).

The *sumu* written 済む means that various problems have been settled like floating objects that have sunk and lie at rest. The example *Koko nite wa ... to mineba sumanu zo* (*Santaishishō*) means that things cannot be settled in this regard without seeing them. Generally, this means that things have finished completely, one has paid off one's debts, and things fall within the expected degree or range. The typical Japanese expression of apology, *sumanai* or *sumimasen*, implies that the speaker will not leave things as they are, that he will not fail to sort them out.

As an extension of the above, 住む (to reside) is explained as follows:

> A cognate of *sumu* (澄). It means that things that move around have settled down and taken root.
>
> (*Iwanami Classical Dictionary*)

This shows that the word 住む (to reside) implies that something floating, twisted, turbulent or incomplete becomes somehow clear and settled, quietly fixed. To employ the previously mentioned terms from Zeami's theory of Noh, it is *jōju* and *rakkyo*. To live quietly is also a characteristic of *omoshiroshi* and *medetashi*.

To repeat myself, this means that, no matter how excruciating or sad life might be, if it is seen as a river flowing, the wind blowing, or birds and insects singing, and articulated as a poignant *mizukara* event, then people will eventually rid themselves of the turbid and the opaque, settle down quietly, and reinvigorate themselves—that is, they can become clear (澄む), complete (済む), and live or reside fully (住む) in an *ichigū* of this universe. The *medetai* celebratory piece of Noh, placed at the start (or sometimes the end) of a Noh performance, shows the primary state of the world—in Zeami's words, the *honpū no sugata* (basic form) or *onozukara no sugata* (*onozukara* form). It is a radical affirmation of the real world.

To state the obvious, reality does not directly represent the *honpū no sugata*. In light of the *awai* between *onozukara* and *mizukara*, *mizukara* can never be divided or reduced into general *onozukara*. To put it in another way, this is not a monism without *awai* of the Tendai Buddhist type (i.e., the argument that reality is itself enlightenment).

This can be seen in the nuances and frequent appearance of the word *arigatashi* (gratitude), as seen in the following quotations:

> *Arigata ya osamaru miyo no narai tote* (How grateful for the peaceful reign). (*Nurturing the Aged*)
>
> *Arigata ya kumoi haruka ni misonawasu* (How grateful to see the faraway clouds). (*Nurturing the Aged*)
>
> *Yokuyoku kikeba arigata ya* (In listening carefully, I feel grateful). (*Takasago*)
>
> *Kimi no megumi zo arigataki* (I am grateful for your blessings). (*Takasago*)

In Chapter 2 I discussed in detail how *arigatashi* literally means "difficult to exist" concerning something that is rare or infrequently encountered. *Arigatashi* consists of *ari* (exist) and *gatashi* (difficult).

It is based on a feeling that something is revered and delightful because it is rare, which in turn becomes gratitude toward the rarity itself, or toward whatever or whoever made it rare.

Medetashi also celebrates rarity. In our everyday world, the word is used at the New Year or other annual festivals as well as rites of passage to confirm future safety or accomplishments.

Both *medetashi* and *omoshiroshi* imply a promising ray of light for the future while showing appreciation for past safety or accomplishments. This is connected to the last part of Chapter 5, "Sayōnara."

At any rate, it probably goes without saying that a certain *arigatai*, *medetai*, and *omoshiroi* function cannot be perceived or realized without a consciousness or expression of *mujō* and the limitedness of *mizukara*. In other words, *shiawase* is an event that arises between the *awai* of *onozukara* and *mizukara*, as I stated earlier.

CHAPTER 5

The *Awai* between *Onozukara* and *Mizukara*

Is this world a mere dream or is it real? Since we are here and not here, I know not whether it is a dream or not.

(*Kokin wakashū* [Collection of Japanese Poems of Ancient and Modern Times])

Theoretical Framework of the *Awai* between *Onozukara* and *Mizukara*

In this last chapter I will consider the question of the framework of the *awai* between *onozukara* and *mizukara* by confirming the origins of the words *onozukara*, *mizukara*, and *awai*.

> *Onozukara*: nature, universe, necessity/chance, unavoidableness, irresistibility, generation, *mujō*...
>
> *Mizukara*: self, oneself, I, desire, will, wish, effort, human intervention, technology...
>
> *Awai*: correlation, interaction, conflict...

First I would like to give an overview of the theoretical framework; the details will be scrutinized individually later. *Onozukara* is obviously the state of the universe and nature as it is. The ordinary word for "nature"—*shizen* (自然)—was originally an adverb like *gūzen* (偶然; by chance) and *totsuzen* (突然; suddenly), but it became nominalized in the Meiji period. In this nominalization we can see a change in the relationship of modern Japanese people vis-à-vis nature. In any event, *shizen*, like *onozukara*, was used principally as an adverb, sometimes in the sense of "inevitably" and sometimes meaning "coincidentally."

First of all, *onozukara* is a function that can be regarded as natural, inevitable, or coincidental. Birth, aging, sickness, and death, for example, are unavoidable and inexorable. These are the functions of that which creates all beings and at the same time the *mujō* function that causes all beings to change.

Next, we have the *mizukara* acts that are exercised on our own volition. These acts are not limited to human beings, but animals and plants can manage to perform *mizukara* acts as well. However, here *mizukara* is particularly limited to mankind. This is the so-called self, oneself, I, desire, will, wish, or prayer. It is also called human intervention, artifice, contrivance, or technology. Mankind lives in a relationship with *onozukara* and other things while doing such *mizukara* acts.

The word *awai*, which is written with the same kanji as the synonymous *aida* (間; the interval between things) is a more dynamic means of expressing this relationship. Various events in our life can be said to take place in the *awai* where *onozukara* and *mizukara* correlate, interact, or conflict with one another.

Awai as an Issue in Japanese Philosophy

Various Japanese thinkers have taken up the issue of *awai*. For example, in *Nihon bunka no mondai* (Issues of Japanese Culture), Nishida Kitarō states that "we Japanese people strongly yearn for a 'selfless' state of mind in which one simply relies on Buddha, and *mizukara* and *onozukara* are united as one." In his "Nihonteki seikaku" (The Japanese Character), Kuki Shūzō writes that "in the ideals of Japanese morality, *onozukara* nature has special significance." And in *Shi to shi* (Poetry and Death) Karaki Junzō says that "pines maintain perfect composure as pines, and bamboo exists in essence as bamboo…; this is the border where *mizukara* is *onozukara*, and *onozukara* is *mizukara*."

As we saw earlier, Miki Kiyoshi realized that "our acts, while done by ourselves, mean to us what just happens to turn out" (*An Introduction to Philosophy*). Both Isobe Tadamasa's *shizen* (nature) centrism and Sagara Tōru's *onozukara* metaphysics are answers to questions that arise within this same framework.

While *onozukara* and *mizukara* can be written with the same kanji (自; self), it does not follow, as we have already seen, that *onozukara* and *mizukara* are identical. They overlap and deviate, deviate and overlap; this is why the word *awai* is resorted to. Depending on one's view of *awai*, Japanese ideology can be judged as being broad, diverse, and encompassing in nature, or criticized as vague, irresponsible, disordered, or unsystematic.

By taking these problems under consideration once again, I hope we can arrive at a better understanding of both aspects.

Awai as a Standpoint from which to View Contemporary Philosophy

Obviously, the issue of the *awai* between *onozukara* and *mizukara* is not especially limited to the Japanese people. It is a universal question of boundaries that is applicable to everyone who shares in a human existence that is natural and at the same time is not.

In 2008 I organized a symposium titled *Jiku no jidai I / Jiku no jidai II—Ikani mirai o kōsō shiuru ka* (Axial Age I / Axial Age II: How Can We Design the Future?) under the auspices of the thanatology project at the Graduate School of Humanities and Social Sciences, University of Tokyo. I was the coordinator, and the symposium consisted of an address by Mita Munesuke with comments by panelists Katō Norihiro, Taguchi Randy, Takeda Seiji, and Shimazono Susumu. The discussion focused on the major philosophical problems of our day. I would like to provide an overall picture of the event since several important points were raised. In the keynote address, Mita made the following proposal:

1. The number of particular members of certain species in certain environmental conditions basically constitutes the S-shaped curve called a logistic curve that goes through a gradual proliferation phase and then a mass proliferation phase. When it nears the limit of environmental capacity, the proliferation slows down and goes into a stable equilibrium stage. The human species in the global environment is also subject to this limitation. The future of the human species depends on how we go beyond the S-shaped curve and shift into the stable equilibrium period.
2. For these last one hundred years, global energy consumption has been accelerating in the form of an almost right-angle curve. However, it has nearly reached its limit in terms of resources and environ-

ment. If we do not decelerate at some time, the human species will have no future.

3. In the spiritual history of mankind there is a period called the Axial Age, when the pivotal thinking that continues up to the present day was created, including Greek philosophy, Buddhism, Confucianism, and Christianity (Axial Age I). Now, however, we must create new ways of thinking (a virtual Axial Age II) to respond to the conditions mentioned above. This challenge means we need to establish an intellectual framework and a social system to effectively respond to the limitations of the world today.
4. Humanism cannot survive except with a philosophy that goes beyond humanism.
5. The above ideological problems should be addressed only after acquiring an accurate understanding of the ongoing transformation in people's consciousness that has been taking place since the 1970s.

("Symposium Address: *Axial Age I / Axial Age II: How Can We Design the Future?*")

In short, human civilization will fail if present trends continue. As we have already seen in Chapter 1, this is an issue on everyone's mind. The question is how to approach it.

In his consideration of this issue, Mita introduced a biological model on a logistic curve—that is, a model of the *onozukara* of natural phenomena. In this connection, I think we can see his proposition as a problem of the *mizukara* and how we are going to accept the possibilities of its limitedness.

Humanism is, in a word, *mizukara*-ism. Transcending it seems to depend on how we come to terms with *onozukara*. This is exactly the issue of the *awai* between *onozukara* and *mizukara*.

As mentioned earlier, the incidental issues of environmental ethics and bioethics are basically matters concerning the *awai* between the *onozukara* and *mizukara*. In other words, the *onozukara* and *mizukara* are issues to be correlatively brought into question in regard to the *awai*, not premised on preconceived ideas of the *onozukara* and *mizukara* and questioning them separately. It is not simply a matter of going back to nature or *onozukara*, or surrendering to one's *mizukara* wishes and desires. This point will be scrutinized further in the section on *awai*.

The *Awai* in *Fullmetal Alchemist*

This may seem a digression, but here I would like to take a look at Arakawa Hiromu's manga *Hagane no renkinjutsushi* (Fullmetal Alchemist). A certain magazine asked if I could be interviewed and give my ethical assessment of the manga. Actually I hadn't read it yet, but I was told that it consisted of 27 volumes and that, amazingly, it had sold more than 50 million copies. Since so many young adults and children had read the work, I expected that they would naturally share the mentality and feelings of the characters depicted, including sympathy and antipathy. With these ideas in mind, I agreed to be interviewed.

Alchemy is a subject closely related to *awai*. According to the story, alchemy is a technology based on the principle of "equivalent exchange," which requires a knowledge of process, disintegration, and reassembly. Newton is said to have been an alchemist. The manga features a great deal of SF-like technology, such as ultramodern man-made androids and chimera minions, and skillfully interweaves neo-futuristic science and the mysteries of pre-modern alchemy in its setting.

The issue here is the various ways that *onozukara* nature is being destroyed by *mizukara* technology, the ways that humanity is being devastated. The main character and his brother fail to alchemize their dead mother, and in the process the older brother loses his right arm and left leg, while the younger brother loses all his body and is reduced to a suit of empty armor with his soul inside. In addition to the brothers, various creatures appear, and throughout the work the question of what it means to be human is continually raised.

However, this question does not seem to be one that can be answered by a simple textbook definition—human beings are this or that and nothing more or less. It is not a question that can be easily answered according to a manual. The tendency to turn to manuals, ready-made definitions, or academic distinctions seems to be an extremely simplistic and dangerous approach, which is also seen in the recent demand for a uniform guideline regarding end-of-life care and the determination of brain death.

The question of "what is man" has always been one of the central questions of philosophy, including the field of ethics, and it has been raised not only in Japan but worldwide. Needless to say, a simplistic definition might have the adverse effect of expanding the area that is considered to be nonhuman.

One Japanese folktale tells of a woman who married and gave birth to a child, but it was discovered, when a dog kept barking at her, that she was in fact a fox. After the woman/fox departed, her husband was so lonely for her that he wept his heart out. There is also a similar folktale called *Shinoda zuma* (The Wife of Shinoda), which relates the love of the occultist Abe no Seimei for his fox mother. The question here is how we should regard the existence of such beings.

Simple distinctions as to what is human and what is not don't help us to understand, for example, Buddhist metempsychosis, where a cow standing in front of me might have been my father in a previous life, or that my wife was once a turtle or a crane. Rather than adopting simplistic distinctions, the key question here is what they mean for us. While enjoying such folklore, we can contemplate them and gain an understanding about the relationship between human beings and other creatures.

The question in *Fullmetal Alchemist* requires not stereotypical answers but serious consideration of how we should see and treat such existences. *Awai* provides an effective and necessary means of answering this question.

Intimately related to this issue, *Fullmetal Alchemist* also raises questions about modern cloning technology and artificial manipulation of human life, making death and immortality another important theme. The story starts with the brothers' failure to alchemize their dead mother, and as I mentioned earlier, the work is populated by chimeras, androids, ghosts, and entities called homunculi that have been living for hundreds of years. In one way or another, both alchemy and Taoist elixirs of life (which also make an appearance) aim at immortality. This is also true of modern cloning technology, which is depicted as a symbol of *mizukara*'s striving to supersede *onozukara*.

Recent scientific findings reveal that lethal genes are present in the cells of living creatures that program the cells to die after the lapse of a certain period of time. However, cancer cells do not have such lethal genes, so they are said to be immortal. To put it another way, life contains death, and that is the nature of *onozukara*. In this sense, those who are immortal do not live a life truly worthy of the name.

There is an episode in the manga where an overly ambitious alchemist inadvertently alchemizes his daughter with a dog and turns her into a chimera. Even though chimeras cannot die, in one scene she murmurs, "I want to die." This remark is made in all seriousness. Amazingly, Arakawa addresses weighty themes like this in a manga format. I felt that he was questioning the nature of human desire.

In June 2010 the *Fullmetal Alchemist* series was concluded. In an interview with the *Asahi Shimbun*, Arakawa said, "At the beginning, when I thought about what the protagonist would gain from the story, I realized that there was something he didn't need." He went on to say that that something was "what could be referred to as his identity. He forfeited the significance of his existence" (*Hito to wa nanika kangaeta kyūnen: Ninki manga "Hagane no renkinjutsushi" kanketsu* [Nine Years Thinking about "What Is Mankind?": Popular Manga "Fullmetal Alchemist" Concluded], *Asahi Shimbun*, June 18, 2010). As the final words of the creator of this work, I felt they were imbued with deep feeling.

The Meanings of *Onozukara* and *Mizukara*

Now that we have surveyed the conceptual framework of *awai* and its historical and modern scope, I would next like to examine the content of *onozukara* and *mizukara* by tracing their origins and history as words.

Onozukara is explained in the *Iwanami Classical Dictionary* as follows:

> *Onozukara* (naturally, spontaneously)
> Means 己つ柄 (*ono-tsu-kara*). [*Ono* means "itself."] *Tsu* [*zu*] is an attributive particle. *Kara* means "inborn."
>
> 1. Natural power. Inborn power.
>   *Yamanoe no ishi no mii wa onozukara nareru nishiki o hareru yama kamo* (The fountain of Ishi at Yamanoe has magnificent scenery like *onozukara* brocade).
>   (*Man'yōshū*)
>   *Kono kotoba no uta no yō naru wa, kajitori no onozukara no kotoba nari* (These words, which sound like a song, resounded like the *onozukara* words of the boatmen). (*Tosa nikki* [Tosa Diary])
> 2. In a natural course. Naturally. (Through the development of events) inevitably.
>   *Anagachi ni (kōi o) omaesarazu motenasasetamai-*

> *shi hodo ni onozukara karoki katachi nimo mieshi o*
> (Because the emperor refused to allow the lady to leave him, she *onozukara* looked like a woman of a low rank). *(The Tale of Genji)*

3. Letting the matter take its own course.
4. By chance. Casually.
   > *Onozukara ki nado mo suru hito no sudare no uchi ni hitobito amata arite mono nado iu ni* (A person came *onozukara*, and many ladies were chatting behind the bamboo blind).
   > *(Makura no sōshi* [The Pillow Book])
5. (With words representing subjunctive conditions or presumption) Perhaps. Maybe.
   > *(Jijō wa) onozukara kikoshimeshikemu* (Perhaps he has heard [of the situation] *onozukara*).
   > *(The Tale of Genji)*

Onozukara shares *kara* (inborn) with several other words: for example, *yakara* (clan) and *harakara* (sibling) as well as *kunigara* (national character) and *iegara* (family lineage). In short, it means "inborn and natural," and is understood to mean "without human manipulation" or "just as it is." *Onozukara* is used both as a noun and adverb. The *Iwanami Classical Dictionary* gives five meanings for *onozukara*, as indicated above. It is worth mentioning here, however, that meanings #3, #4, and #5 are not in use today. In any case, all imply that the action in question was not carried out *mizukara*.

In contrast to *onozukara*, the origin of the word *mizukara* is as follows:

> *Mizukara* (自ら)
> Literally means 身つから (*mi-tsu-kara*).
> [*Mi* means one's self or one's body.] *Tsu* [*zu*] is an attributive particle. *Kara* means inborn nature.
>
> 1. (Noun) Self, one's own self. Indicates the person himself regardless of grammatical person.
> 2. (Pronoun) The first person. I.
> 3. (Adverb) On one's own.
>   *Kōge o mochite issai no shobutsu ni kuyō shitatematsure. Mizukara sono tsumi o chinseyo* (Hold a memorial service and attend to all the buddhas. Confess one's own guilt on one's own.) (*Konkōmyō-saishōōkyō* [Golden Light Sutra])
>
> (*Iwanami Classical Dictionary*)

Mizukara and *onozukara* are similar in origin but still different. The main difference is that *mi* means "body" or "one's self," while *ono* means "itself." As shown in the quotation cited above—"Confess your own guilt on your own"—*mizukara* is used to signify "willingly," "consciously," or "with one's own thought, will, feeling, desire or effort." *Onozukara*, on the other hand, means things turn out on their own, unconsciously or before one notices, without will or effort. In this regard, *onozukara* and *mizukara* are obviously different.

The Ambiguity of *Onozukara*

As we saw earlier, the word *onozukara*, with a central meaning of "naturally," means "necessarily" and "as a matter of course" on the one hand and "coincidentally" on the other. I would now like to look into the subtle differences between these two meanings by examining specific texts.

Here I will turn to the 13th-century *Shin kokin wakashū* (New Collection of Ancient and Modern Japanese Poetry). It contains many poems with the word *onozukara*, of which I will examine five.

1. *Onozukara suzushiku mo aru ka natsugoromo hi mo yūgure no ame no nagori ni* (It has become cool *onozukara* thanks to the remnant of the evening shower we had while I was tying up the summer clothing).
2. *Onozukara oto-suru mono wa niwa no mo ni konoha fukimaku tani no yūkaze* (The *onozukara* sound of the evening wind from the valley scatters leaves in the garden).
3. *Onozukara iwanu o shitau hito aru ya to yasurau hodo ni toshi no kurenuru* (The year ended while I was hesitating whether there was *onozukara* someone who through love would visit this mountain village, though I dared not ask him to visit me).
4. *Onozukara sakoso are to omou ma ni makoto ni hito no towazu narinuru* (Although I am prepared for it *onozukara*, he really keeps away from me).

5. *Asu shiranu inochi o zo omou onozukara araba au yo matsu ni tsukete mo* (While waiting for tomorrow, I feel I may not be alive then, but if I am *onozukara* still living, my dream to meet together will be fulfilled).

Poem #1 says that the remnant of the evening, after it showered, was inevitably and naturally cool. No contingency is included here.

Poem #2 says that the only sound to be heard is the evening wind from the valley blowing against the leaves of the trees and making them rustle *onozukara*. Therefore, the sound can be interpreted as a natural event, simply the result of the wind blowing against the leaves of the trees. However, it can also be interpreted to mean that although it is usually quiet, the wind happened to blow, hitting against the leaves of the trees and making a sound. In this sense, naturalness, inevitableness, and coincidence can be read in the use of *onozukara*.

In poem #3, *onozukara* modifies *shitau hito aru ya* ("whether there was someone who through love"). This poem means that while she was hesitating whether there was someone who would *onozukara* love her and come to visit though she had not extended an invitation, the year ended. This *onozukara* is quite delicate. It can be interpreted as meaning that he naturally did not come because she hesitated to invite him, or she decided not to invite him out of decorum though she secretly expected that he would perhaps love her and visit her. This is quite ambiguous wording.

The same is true of poem #4. It says that while she thought *onozukara* that it might happen, he really did stop visiting her. This *onozukara* can be interpreted as "while she thought it might naturally happen," or "while she thought it might contingently happen."

Poem #5 says, "I feel I may not be alive then, but if I am *onozukara* still living," so the part containing *onozukara* obviously means "if I am by chance alive." This usage of *onozukara* with the implication of "by chance" became common from this period onward.

As we have seen above, the usage of the word *onozukara* at that time had the ambiguous meanings of necessarily/naturally and coincidentally. By way of contrast with *onozukara*, here is an excerpt from the "Kana Preface" of the *New Collection of Ancient and Modern Japanese Poetry* in which *mizukara* and *tezukara* ("with one's own hand") appear:

> *Sonoue, mizukara sadame, tezukara migakeru koto wa…*
> *Konouchi, mizukara no uta o nosetaru koto, furuki tagui wa aredo, jūshu ni wa sugizaru beshi* (Moreover, the case when the emperor *mizukara* decided and *tezukara* selected… In old anthologies the emperors who commissioned the compilation included their own poems, but the number was not more than ten).

Here *mizukara* is used as a synonym for, and in apposition to, *tezukara*, meaning to do something with one's own hands instead of having others do it. This shows that *mizukara* means "willingly," according to one's own thought or volition. In contrast, *onozukara* is a function that makes things turn out without our noticing it, unconsciously, on their own.

As a synonym of *onozukara*, I will confirm the meaning of the word *shizen* in the following from the *Iwanami Classical Dictionary*:

> Shizen
> 1. Being *onozukara*.
> 2. (Representing a situation that is humanly impossible to change) Contingency. Eventuality.
>
>> *Kono gosho wa bunai semaku shite shizen no koto aran toki ashikaru beshi* (This court site is so narrow that it could cause a problem in the event of a *shizen* occurrence). (*Hōgen monogatari* [The Tale of Hōgen])
>>
>> *Shizen, Kamakura ni ondaiji araba* (Shizen [by chance], if an important affair happens in Kamakura).
>> (*Hachinoki* [The Potted Trees; a Noh play])

This meaning is exactly the same as that of *onozukara*. In meaning #1, *shizen* means natural, unavoidable, or inevitable, but in meaning #2 it refers to a situation that is humanly impossible to change, an eventuality, or contingency with a higher probability than normal. *Shizen no koto aran toki* means "in the event of a contingency." Here we can see that *shizen* was used with an implication of "if worst comes to worst."

Onozukara as Otherness

Onozukara and *shizen* often appear in military epics from the middle ages. The following are some examples from *Heike monogatari* (The Tale of the Heike) and *Gikeiki* (The Chronicle of Yoshitsune):

1. *Konotabi no ikusa ni, otoko no inochi no ikinokoran koto wa, senman ga hitotsu mo arigatashi. Tatoi mata tōkiyukari wa, onozukara ikinokoru koto ari to iu tomo...* (In the next battle, there is a tiny chance that men will survive. Even should distant relatives *onozukara* survive...) (*The Tale of the Heike*)
2. *San no toki shizen no koto araba...*" (In the case of a *shizen* happening at the time of birth...) (*The Chronicle of Yoshitsune*)

Example #1 means that in the next battle, there is only a tiny chance that men will survive, even if distant relatives should escape death *onozukara*. *Onozukara* here refers to the contingency of "a tiny chance." Example #2 means "If I had perchance died while giving birth." Both indicate the uncertainties of life and death.

Nowadays we have lost these nuances, but in the uncertainty of *onozukara* and *shizen* the ancient Japanese still retained a sense of the workings of chance, particularly in questions of life and death, not to mention their inevitability and naturalness.

The wisdom here is to accept what we feel to be contingent as natural and inevitable from the standpoint of heaven and earth or the universe. *Onozukara* and *shizen* represent those things that cannot be helped, despite our desires and hopes, and so they can be viewed as natural and inevitable as well as accidental and contingent.

The *onozukara* functions of *shizen* show that they operate as overriding forces, regardless of us, though we are certainly inside those functions.

Shinran's religious thought can be considered as being based on *onozukara*, which he refers to as *jinen* in the following excerpt where the word is written with the same kanji as *shizen* (自然):

> *Ji* in *jinen* means *onozukara*, which is not based on the aspirations of a Buddhist novice. It means to cause to happen. *Nen* also means to cause to happen regardless of the intent of the Buddhist novice.... The word *jinen* therefore means basically to cause to happen.
> (*Last Letters of Shinran*)

The *onozukara* functions of *jinen* at work in the world far surpass our own wishes. In this world, doing good things does not necessarily bring about good results, while doing bad things does not necessarily bring about bad results. Shinran tries to see the functions of the all-saving Amida Buddha precisely in the *onozukara* functions of *jinen* that surpass human effort. This requires belief in this function and the ritual chanting of a prayer (*nenbutsu*) to Amida Buddha. However, neither this belief nor the chanting of the *nenbutsu* are viewed as spontaneous *mizukara* acts or as being compelled by *onozukara*; they are regarded by

Shinran as functions to be sought in the *awai* between *onozukara* and *mizukara*.

As I have repeatedly said, this is because the existence and acts of *mizukara* are both inside and outside *onozukara*'s existence and functions. In Chapter 1, we saw this in Kiyozawa Manshi's words, "We should not overlook the fact that *mugen* and *yūgen* are of the same body, and that at the same time *mugen* exists outside *yūgen*."

Sakaguchi Ango's View of *Onozukara*

Here I would like to look at a concrete example showing that *mizukara* is both inside and outside *onozukara*, and that the two are separate things. The following represents Sakaguchi Ango's basic way of thinking about literature.

> A pretty girl—pleasant, tender, virtuous, free from all evil—visits her sick grandmother in the forest and is eaten up by a wolf disguised as the grandmother.
>
> We suddenly feel—do we not?—alienated from the scene, as if this was not the way it was supposed to be, incredulous, pushed into a tenuous void, an extremely quiet but transparent place, the plaintive home of our hearts, our *furusato*....
>
> There is an anecdote about Akutagawa Ryūnosuke in his later years. One day a peasant writer, one of the poorest of the poor, brought a manuscript for Akutagawa to look over. When Akutagawa read it, he saw

it was about a peasant whose wife had just given birth, but since the peasant was so poor, he decided it would be best for everyone if he killed the child and disposed of it in an oil drum.

The story was unbearably gloomy and unimaginable from Akutagawa's perspective, so he asked if such things really happened.

Gruffly the peasant answered that that was exactly what he had done. The thought was so terrible that Akutagawa was at a loss for words. In the same gruff voice the peasant asked him if he had done wrong....

After the peasant departed Akutagawa's study, leaving behind this incontrovertible "fact," Akutagawa suddenly felt cut off from the world, all alone....

Once upon a time, a man fell in love with a woman and earnestly courted her, but she wouldn't say yes. At last, after three years, she said she would marry him, causing him to jump with joy. They decided to elope and flee the city. After they had passed a place called Akuta no Watashi and entered a field, evening fell, thunder clapped, and it began to rain. The man took the woman by the hand and began to run across the field. Seeing dew on the grass lit by the lightning, she asked, "What is that?" But the man was in such a hurry that he couldn't manage an answer. At last they found a deserted house and rushed inside. He thrust her in a closet, in front of which he stationed himself with a spear in hand to ward off any demons. Nevertheless, a

5: *Awai* between *Onozukara* and *Mizukara*

demon did come and ate her in the closet. The thunder was so fierce that the man didn't hear her scream. Only at the break of day did he realize that she had been killed by a demon. Weeping, he wrote a poem:

Nubatama no nanika to hito no toishi toki tsuyu to kotaete kienamashi mono o. (When the woman asked what it was when she saw dew on the grass leaves, I should have answered it was dew and disappeared at once.)

The gem-like coldness that these three stories convey is something like absolute loneliness—the loneliness inherent in existence itself....

Here I see the *furusato* (ancestral home) of literature or of all mankind. Literature starts from here—that is my belief.

I don't mean to say that only such amoral, detached stories constitute literature. In fact, I do not value these stories that highly. This is because although our *furusato* is the cradle of our lives, it is not by any means the task of adult people to return to our *furusato*....

However, I do not think that literature can come into existence where there is no awareness or consciousness of this *furusato*. I never trust the morality or sociality of literature unless it has emerged from this ancestral home. I believe the same is true of literary criticism.

(*Bungaku no furusato* [The Ancestral Home of Literature])

To summarize, Ango sensed in these stories a preternatural coldness, the inherent loneliness of existence itself, which he named, in his own unique way, "the *furusato* of literature, or the birthplace of mankind."

No matter what good things or bad things we do, there is a sphere of events beyond the reach of morality, commitment, or meaning. It is consistently amoral in itself, so it is referred to as absolute loneliness or coldness, or, as he says elsewhere, as nihility and meaningless nonsense. We feel suddenly as if we have been cut off from the normal, "as if this is not the way things are supposed to be." However, Ango says this is our true home.

Furusato is originally the place where we were born and came into the world, but Ango says that it simultaneously thrusts us away. This is exactly the presence of the *onozukara* that we originally emerged from but which is still alien to us.

Following his statement, "I don't mean to say that only amoral, detached stories constitute literature," he goes on to say that human beings cannot live with *onozukara* alone since it is alien to us. He explains that we always make commitments, build morals, and create stories in relation to *mizukara* precisely because we cannot live solely with absolute loneliness.

In the story of the man eloping with a woman, when she sees dew on the grass and asks what it is, he regrets not replying that it was dew and saying that they should disappear with it. This, Ango believes, is where the true meaning of literature and life lie.

To repeat, it is the *mizukara* act that identifies cold solitude and nihility with the *furusato*. In other words, what exists in the *awai* between *onozukara* and *mizukara* is real literature, or what is called morality and social life.

Omnipresent *Onozukara* and Partial *Mizukara*

The question of the *awai*, where *mizukara* is *onozukara* and at the same time is not, is a central issue in the thought of Ninomiya Sontoku (1787–1856). Sontoku was not an armchair academic, but actually undertook efforts to rebuild communities in run-down villages, developing a unique approach that focused on the *awai* between the functions of nature and mankind.

The basic image of Ninomiya's perspective of the world is as follows:

> By nature, a cloud has no roots, no branches, no hands or feet, no corners round or square, no place to reside or come to rest; it proceeds and moves by the power of the wind in the disk of the sky. Without moving or resting on its own, without coming or going on its own, without sitting calmly or walking out on its own, it simply waits for the wind.
>
> (*Godō sōan* [Preliminary Thoughts on the Path to Enlightenment])

The "cloud" here is a symbol of the status of all worldly things. Everything flows and circulates, like a cloud moved by the wind, without a specific form, coming and going freely. "There is heaven and earth as well as yin and yang. Yang makes things grow and yin makes things quiet down and die. Yin and yang flow, and everything emerges and declines, never ceasing to circulate; spring gives birth, autumn desiccates, fire burns what is dry, and water flows low. They move day and night, but never change" (*Night Chats with Old Man Ninomiya*).

Moreover, this flow and circulation is referred to as movement in the *awai* that Sontoku calls *niken* (二間; "two gaps"), the boundary where two things come and go.

> In the gap between heaven and earth, things emerge from infinitude and decline into finitude. What is not of heaven and not of earth, what emerges and declines but does not become depleted, this is called *niken*. Human beings (*ningen*; "people in the gap") are not the only beings living in this space.
> (*Banbutsu hatsugenshū* [Remarks on All Things])

Not only mankind but all creation—the finite and the infinite, heaven and earth, yin and yang, man and woman—emerges and declines but is not depleted within the *niken*. "The essence of the existence of all creation is the gap called *ma* (間; also pronounced *ken* or *gen*). This is especially true of living things. Everything is made possible only in the gap where the energy (*ki*) of yin and yang rises and falls and the quintessential elements of heaven and earth connect with one another" (Shitahodo Yūkichi, *Tendō to jindō* [Heaven's Way and Man's Way]).

Tendō (Heaven's Way) and *Tenri* (Heaven's Principle: i.e., the laws of nature), as advocated by Ninomiya, are based on a perception of the world that flows and circulates in the *niken*; but of course, not everything in the world exists only in the phase of flow and circulation.

> All beings emerge by partialization.... If not partialized, they cannot keep their true nature....
>
> If a person is born, there is celebration, and if a person dies, he goes back to emptiness. It is as if we make a tub and pour water into it. If the tub is broken, then the water goes back to the earth. Therefore, heaven and earth have been filled with celebration since the beginning of time.
> (*Ninomiya sensei goroku* [Analects of Master Ninomiya])

Beings cannot exist if they only flow and circulate. They come to exist with form because there is a certain partiality. Ninomiya says that "if not partialized, they cannot keep their true nature." Human beings exist like a tub of water. The general idea is that, if a person dies, the "tub" is broken and what was partialized there returns to heaven and earth.

This is the fundamental metaphysics of Ninomiya Sontoku. He says that it is because of the partialization and concentration of the flowing and circulating of the universal *onozukara* that all beings come to exist; this applies especially to human beings, who are partialized into "the personal being called the self." For him, *mizukara* is the partialization of the omnipresent *onozukara*.

> The world is a wide place, so we should be broadminded.

> However, if we look at that world from the perspective of the personal being called the self, the world's reason becomes removed from that self and we only see half the reality. (*Night Chats with Old Man Ninomiya*)

That is, to take the unique perspective of *mizukara* means to adopt a position, and that is where the *awai* emerges.

For "the personal being called the self," *Jindō* (the Way of Man) is composed as something that is good. "*Jindō* is the place where Man stands" (*Night Chats with Old Man Ninomiya*). If we simply leave things to the Way of Heaven (*Tendō*), we cannot grow crops in the fields. Millet and weeds are bad; rice and wheat are good. *Jindō* comes into effect when we purposefully grow and harvest the good alone. This is an intentional, proactive *mizukara* act. The important point in Ninomiya's thought and practice is that he views the relationship of these acts to the *onozukara* as follows:

> The Way of Man is like a waterwheel. Half of it follows the water current; the other half turns against it. If the wheel is entirely under the water, it does not turn and will be swept away. On the other hand, it cannot move entirely away from the water.... Therefore, the Way of Man respects moderation. The moderation of a waterwheel lies in its being under water to an appropriate degree, half following the current and half turning against it, so that the wheel keeps working without getting stuck. Similarly, man should sow seeds follow-

ing the laws of nature and remove weeds against the laws of nature, working diligently at the family business according to one's desires while controlling these desires in order to fulfill one's duty.

(*Night Chats with Old Man Ninomiya*)

The "appropriate degree" in the sentence above refers to the *awai*. Partialized *mizukara* can "keep working without getting stuck" only in the *awai*, where it moves half with and half against the flowing *onozukara*. Here lies the principle behind Ninomiya's thought concerning various types of practical reform.

Solidification of *Mizukara* and the Problem of the "I"

It should be unnecessary to point out that Ninomiya Sontoku's argument on the *awai* is essentially different from the dualism of the modern West, in which the cognitive actor perceives the object in a dualistic way. However, in modern Japan, which underwent rapid Western modernization, *mizukara* lost its *awai*-ness with *onozukara* and became nominally fixed and enlarged in meaning. Accordingly, *onozukara* (*shizen*) also became nominally fixed (as a translation of "nature"), and lost its original mobility.

I took up various recent issues and events concerning the modern self in my previous book, *Jikochōetsu no shisō: Kindai Nihon no nihirizumu* (The Philosophy of Self-Transcendence: Nihilism in Modern Japan), so I will not repeat the same argument here, but the main point can be understood from the following:

> The idea that we humans cannot peacefully survive without solidificating ourselves—that is the root of all nihilism.
>
> (Kimura Bin, *Gūzensei no seishin byōri* [The Psychopathology of Contingency])

We have already discussed Kimura's simple metaphor comparing *mizukara* to the arch of a current of water that spurts out under the pressure of *onozukara*. This overlaps with the origin of the word *inochi* (life), which is also pushed out by the fundamental force of the "momentum of breath." However, he points out here that we tend to think that *mizukara* cannot prosper without detaching it from *onozukara* and consolidating and solidificating it. Therein, he says, lies the root of all nihilism. It is this situation that leads to the loss of *awai*.

This, I believe, is a momentous problem.

Kimura's proposition that we humans cannot peacefully survive without solidificating ourselves is, in a sense, indisputably true of all times and places, not restricted to modern Japan. This is similar to Ninomiya Sontoku's statement that "All beings emerge by partialization.... If not partialized, they cannot keep their true nature." All beings are born by partialization, and mankind is especially fixated on partialization, Sontoku writes. The personal being called the self exists because man clings to it like water in a tub.

I would now like to turn my attention to the issue of *watashi* (私) and *ware* (我), both meaning "one's self" or "I."

私: Originally composed of 禾 (rice plant) and 厶 (enclosure). Means rice plants that one has enclosed and made one's own.

(*Kanjigen* [The Origin of Chinese Characters])

我: Originally modeled on a type of pike with a saw-toothed head. (*The Origin of Chinese Characters*)

As we can see from the above, these two kanji were used to indicate one's self. One, 私 (*watashi*), meant rice plants that one had enclosed and made one's own; the other, 我 (*ware*), was modeled on a pike and meant the armed self. "I" is said to have emerged through a *mizukara* effort to enclose and possess.

Buddhism singles out this state of mind as evil thought and ignorance, and considers it the source of sin and suffering. In other words, "the root of all nihilism" lies in the plight of 私 and 我.

However, it would be unrealistic here to take up a discussion of this formalistic and abstract non-self doctrine since it amounts, in terms of the present context, to the disintegration of *mizukara* into *onozukara*. In fact, in the history of Buddhist theory, such thinking has been developed in considerable detail. We cannot go into these discussions here, but they include, for example, issues such as the following, which is stated as a rebuttal:

> If our hearts are filled with joyful happiness and we wish to hurry to the Pure Land, we might be mistakenly led to believe that we are free of all earthly desires.
> (*Tannishō*, Article 9)

Chanting the *nenbutsu* does not fill us with joyful happiness nor make us wish to hurry to the Pure Land. This is indeed because of our earthly desires. However, since Amida Buddha, knowing this full well, has pledged to save all beings, we should understand that "going to paradise is predetermined" precisely because we have earthly desires.

The paradoxical expression that "we might be mistakenly led to think that we are free of all earthly desires," represents, I believe, a profound insight into, or resignation concerning, the actuality of human existence—that human beings are "ignorant" and have no choice but to cling to 私 in their lives.

Shinran has a clear perception of 私 that is saved by an act of faith lying beyond resignation.

> When I meditated the prayer of Amida Buddha through five kalpas of profound meditation, it was only for me, Shinran. I am an entity with a variety of karma, and I am so grateful to the Original Vow for saving me.
> (*Tannishō*)

This is a recognition of nothing other than 私, the single individual, which is sensed in Shinran's attempt to entrust his whole existence to Amida Buddha. This recognition is not eliminated by *onozukara* (Amida Buddha) nor independent of *onozukara*; it emerges at the *awai* between *onozukara* and *mizukara*.

As we saw earlier, this is a question of the one-time-only nature of *mizukara*, its irreplaceability, and I would like to confirm that *mizukara* in such cases does not reduce to *onozukara* by demolishing and eliminating *mizukara*, but each entity realizes the operation of its *mizukara* in the *awai* vis-à-vis *onozukara*. I believe this refers to the "emptiness is form" in "form is emptiness; emptiness is form" (*shikisokuzekū kūsokuzeshiki*).

Awai

Up to this point we have examined *onozukara* and *mizukara* in some detail. Lastly, while reconfirming our understanding of the word *awai*, I would now like to consider the practical role that ethics plays in the *awai* between *onozukara* and *mizukara*.

First let us consider *aida*, which is a synonym for *awai* in that it signifies the distance or relationship between things. I have purposely used the term *awai* instead of *aida* because *awai* has a dynamic connotation that *aida* does not possess. Originally, the basic meaning of *aida* indicated, to put it briefly, a somewhat static distance or relationship: in terms of space, "a void between contiguous things," and in terms of time, "a stoppage or repose during continuous movement" (*Iwanami Classical Dictionary*). *Awai*, on the other hand, has a dynamic connotation that is explained as follows:

> *Awai*
> Abbreviation of *ai-ai*. The space between facing things. It has shifted to mean the relationship between two things.
>
> 1. Space between two opposing things.

2. Mutual relationship between two (or more) things.
   (i) Coloration. Proportionality. Used for coloration of clothing etc.
   Sodeguchi no awai warō kasanetaru hito (A person whose sleeve edges overlap with bad coloration).
   (*Murasaki Shikibu nikki* [The Diary of Lady Murasaki])
   (ii) Relationship between people. Terms.
   (*Genji to Murasaki-no-ue wa) ge ni medetaki on-awai domo nari* ([Genji and Lady Murasaki] have a truly blessed relationship.) (*The Tale of Genji*)
   (*Genji to Gennaishi no suke) nitsukahashikaranu awai kana* ([Genji and Gennaishi no Suke] do not have a decent relationship.) (*The Tale of Genji*)
   (iii) Gap. Interval.
   (*Iwanami Classical Dictionary*)

As indicated above, *awai* is an abbreviation of *ai-ai*, a combination of two *ai*, which is the continuative form of *au* [to meet], and means the mutual relationship between two things facing each other. (The *Shogakukan Complete Japanese Language Dictionary* adopts the hypothesis that *ai-ai* is a nominalization of *ahafu* [old spelling of *awau*], which is a combination of the verb *afu* and the suffix *fu*.)

In other words, the word *awai* has the basic meaning of the space between two opposing things, which are obviously two different things. It represents the dynamic condition or relationship of synergy or friction when the two opposing things overlap and cross each other, or go against each other where they encounter one another. For example, to investigate the relationship between A and B in the *awai* does not mean to question the distance (*aida*) between them after determining their contours. It means to inquire into their dynamic correlation, where A expresses A's existence in the *awai* against B, and B does likewise against A. As seen in the examples, it means to acquire anew into both entities and their relationship in terms of coloration, shading, and balance, which sets each off individually.

While in the above we have conducted our discussion in terms of the *awai* between *onozukara* and *mizukara*, this does not mean that we should regard the *awai* as a dichotomy of opposing nouns, such as the concepts of nature and self or nature and artificiality. *Onozukara* and *mizukara* were originally adverbs and adjectives, which did not signify an entity. What we need is to reconsider is the correlation of the two in terms of *awai*.

Further Discussion of "It Turns Out that We Will Get Married"

I have employed the expression "It turns out that we will get married" several times as an example of the *awai* between *onozukara* and *mizukara*. I have pointed out that the expression connotes the awareness that what one did *mizukara* has turned out to possess an *onozukara* aspect. This can lead to the idea of there being no one responsible for *mizukara* behavior. At the same time, however, it also expresses a sensitive gratitude for functions that work beyond the control of *mizukara*, including encountering a marriage partner and various subsequent events.

Consider the word *chigiri*, which is sometimes used in reference to marriage. While, on the one hand, *chigiri* means promises and vows that are the will of the self or *mizukara*, on the other hand it also means fate from a previous life, or karma; that is, the two people are in this relationship as a result of the various karmas from their previous lives. This is very similar to "It turns out that we will get married."

As for the idea that events occur neither by *mizukara* power alone nor by leaving them solely to *onozukara*, but occur in the *awai* in between, the cultural anthropologist Nishie Masayuki (1937–2015) interestingly says that "chance encounters depend on capability." This means that we cannot have a real "encounter" with someone or something without possessing a certain amount of *mizukara* knowledge and sensitivity. If one encounters a picture or some music and feels that it is excellent, this requires some effort on our part—that is, a capability that is the accumulation of such effort. He says that one cannot have *onozukara* encounters or fated meetings without *mizukara* effort or capability. This is a clever expression of the idea of the *awai* that I have discussed so far.

On the difficulty of having an encounter and the *mizukara* effort required, here is a paraphrase of Kiyozawa Manshi's thinking:

> The attainment of belief in Amida Buddha is, for example, like an "encounter" with the moon. We cannot control whether the moon will appear from behind a mountain or not. However, this does not necessarily mean that there is nothing to be done on our part. We

must raise our eyes and keep looking at the fringe of the mountain. Unless we do so, we will not be able to detect the moon when it comes out.

As I have previously discussed in some detail, happiness (*shiawase*) is only possible when we properly accept an encounter—that is, fortune or luck, including prayers or wishes made to the gods or Buddha—which is based on our *mizukara* efforts to "fit in" and be in alignment with *onozukara*.

The Ethics of the *Awai*

While, as stated earlier, we can find the value or significance of *shiawase* (happiness), *tōtoi* (preciousness), or *omoshiroshi* (interest) in the *awai* in some form or other, this does not exclude the existence of an ethical component vis-à-vis neighboring others.

That is, *awai* also includes our attitude toward others. It represents the conditions or relationships in the space between two opposing things, where they intersect and encounter each other. According to the *Iwanami Classical Dictionary*, *awai* means interpersonal relationship. In this sense, *awai* contains an ethical component.

For example, the traditional Japanese ethos is to negate individual *mizukara* and to relate fully and purely with others or the community. However, I believe that this is somewhat different in nature from the *awai* ethic being discussed here. There are important ethical principles like "sincerity," "purity of heart," "honesty," and "selflessness" that should be considered in their own right, but in fact their purpose is the elimination of *awai*.

The ethics of accepting *awai* as *awai* is outlined by Kuki Shūzō as follows:

> An entity that exists alone must feel the distress and joy of all its existence in internalizing the other within the depths of itself the instant it contingently encounters others here and there.... The dualistic relativity that brings contingency into existence structures the fundamental nature of society by revealing intersubjectivity everywhere.
> (*Gūzensei no mondai* [The Problem of Contingency])

Kuki says our existence in this world is fundamentally cotingent. Contingency means an encounter between dualistic, independent entities. In the passage above it refers to the "dualistic relativity" of chance meetings with others. While basing his argument solidly on this understanding of contingency, Kuki thematically addresses the question of how it is possible to interact with others and to create an ethical foundation.

The separating and linking of entity and entity based on dualistic relativity, as well as "internalizing the other," seem to equal the complete acceptance of *awai* as *awai*.

However, this does not mean to unilaterally accept contingency as a given. In *The Problem of Contingency*, for example, this is manifest in the way in which the question of fate is approached. When we feel a certainty in what we have to refer to as contingency, we cannot help thinking about fate as both necessary and contingent (inevitable as well as subject to chance). What is important here is that, since fate is what it is, we should not be caught up in it and tossed about on its waves, but rather we should accept it as it is and embrace it voluntarily through our *mizukara* efforts. It is at this point that it can become our true fate.

Elsewhere Kuki connects this discussion with his long-lasting interest in rhyme in Japanese poetry, which he describes as follows:

> In the face of the mysterious workings of love in this life, it is safe to say that those who do not understand the metaphysical desire to recall how they were united in their previous lives cannot comprehend the essence of rhyme in its depth.
>
> ("Nihonshi no ōin," *Bungeiron*
> ["Rhyme in Japanese Poetry," *On the Literary Arts*])

"Metaphysical desire" does not indicate a desire to impart some substantial meaning to fate or a previous life. Kuki clearly states in *Jinseikan* (The Philosophy of Life): "I myself do not believe in the existence of a next life. If there were a next life, human beings would live twice. It would be as if there were two present lives. Then, the one-time-only nature or preciousness of the present life would start to disintegrate. Our life is transient and fragile, always threatened by death. However, the strength of life itself lies in its transience. All its brilliance and strength lie in the fact that human beings can live only once, and each one of our steps carries us to the ultimate negation of ourselves in death."

In other words, "metaphysical desire," which is the essence of poetry and art, is the advance of our one-time-only contingent steps toward the "eternal now," without the backdrop of a second life in the form of a previous or subsequent existence. Poetic techniques such as rhyme, rhythm, and refrain manifest the "eternal now" by reiterating the "present now." In the paper titled "The Japanese Character," written concurrently with *On the Literary Arts*, Kuki points out that *shizen* (nature), *iki* (sophistication), and *teinen* (resignation) are the three distinctive features of Japanese thought. It can be said that his ethics of structuring the fundamental nature of society "by revealing intersubjectivity everywhere" was envisioned in the *awai* of these distinctive features.

Yasashi

In conclusion, I would like to briefly summarize my thoughts on ethical feelings and salutations such as *yasashi* (gentle), *kanashi* (sad), and *sayōnara* (goodbye), which I have long mulled over as part of the above-mentioned ethics of the *awai*. First comes a discussion of the noun *yasashi* (and its adjectival form *yasashii*) that appears in Dazai Osamu's "Kawamori Yoshizō ate shokan" (Letters to Kawamori Yoshizō):

> I totally agree with your writing the kanji 文化 (*bunka*; culture) with ruby showing that the character is to be read *hanikami* (reserved); i.e., 文化̚ (はにかみ). This makes me think of the kanji 優. It means "excellent," of course, and we see it in such compounds as 優良可 (*yūryōka*; excellent, good, satisfactory grades) and 優勝 (*yūshō*;

victory), but there is another way of reading it, which is *yasashii* (gentle). When we look at this character carefully, we see that it is a combination of a left-hand component meaning "human" and a right-hand component meaning "to grieve." When we grieve over people's troubles and are sensitive to their loneliness, bleakness, or bitterness, we are being *yasashii*. This should make us not only "excellent" people but also somewhat "reserved" in possessing such qualities. I myself am fairly consumed by reservation.

As a matter of fact, without a drink I don't really talk much. In any case, that is the essence of culture, I think. It may seem weak and defeatist, but that is okay, too. I consider myself one of the fallen and alienated. But whether alienated or fallen, isn't it our grumbling about it that produces our literature?

Dazai finds gentleness to be the essence of culture (referring especially to Japanese culture.) He overlaps this with his own literature, saying that *yasashi* exists when we "are sensitive to the loneliness, bleakness, or bitterness" of fragile and defeated people, and that it entails "reservation."

Yasashi comes from *yase*, which is derived from *yaseru* (to lose weight), and its original meaning is evident in the following from the *Iwanami Classical Dictionary*: *(Hitobito no miru me ga ki ni kakatte) mi mo yasehosoru omoi ga suru* (I feels as if I am losing weight [because I'm too sensitive to the way other people look at me]). Also, in the *Man'yōshū* there is: *Yo no naka o ushi to yasa-*

shi to omoedomo tobitachikanetsu tori ni shiaraneba (The world is bitter and I worry about being in the public eye, but I cannot fly away because I am not a bird.) As pointed out in Dazai's passage, weakness, vulnerability, and reserve lie at the root of *yasashi*.

Around the Heian period (794–1185), *yasashi* came to indicate a positive appreciation of diffidence and reserve as sensitive, graceful, and commendable demeanor. In this sense, the word was used as an aesthetic term, but it was not limited to outward appearance. It also indicated a state of mind that was expressed in a reserved, inartificial way.

> How *yasashi*! Who could you be? Your army has taken flight but you fight on alone. So admirable!
> (The Tale of the Heike)

The Heike's old commander Sanemori, who stayed back and fought on after his army had been routed, is praised as *yasashi*. What is important here is that Sanemori was not fighting in a wild frenzy but remained calm and collected. He would not have been praised as *yasashi* otherwise. Sanemori even went so far as to dye his gray hair black to disguise his age, and he perished without revealing his identity, displaying, in a sense, the "reserve" of Dazai. The whole of his conduct is regarded as *yasashi*.

In the 12th to 16th centuries of the late medieval period, the modern-day meanings of "compassionate" and "kind" appeared, but there was always the implication of reserve and proper behavior according to person and situation in order not to embarrass oneself.

This type of *yasashi* demeanor and behavior is always premised to some extent on an awareness of the finiteness and transience of ourselves and others. The linked-verse poet Shinkei (1406–75) expressed it as follows:

> Whenever you see flying petals or falling leaves, or look at the dew on grass and trees, be aware that this world is just an illusion. Make your conduct *yasashi* and keep *yūgen* (the subtle and profound) in mind.
> (*Shinkei hōin teikin* [Priest Shinkei's Domestic Lessons])

Yūgen is one of the terms that represent the aesthetic ideals of the Japanese people. It can be defined as follows: *Yūgen* is "the suggestiveness that does not appear in words; it is an invisible atmosphere" (Kamo no Chōmei, *Mumyōshō* [The Nameless Treatise]).

Yūgen is the suggestiveness that remains when we do not clearly express ourselves in so many words. There are even instances where the kanji for *yūgen* is read *yasashi*, indicating the similarity between the two types of beauty.

It hardly needs saying that this beauty of image and movement is connected to Zeami's words, "If hidden, it is the flower; if not hidden, it cannot be the flower." Here there is an aesthetic of the *awai*, which expresses indirectness rather than directness. It is also an aesthetic of gentle blurring.

Accepting Shinkei's words, "be aware that this world is just an illusion," does not, of course, embrace nihilism, which means everything is void, emptiness, or the nothingness of illusion. It is on the same plane as Sakaguchi Ango's thought that literature, society, and ethics can only exist in painful *mizukara* acts in an unmalleable *onozukara*. Even though Sakaguchi realizes that this is a world of illusion, seeing the dew, he asks and tells what it is. In other words, *yūgen* and *yasashi* appear in how we relate (connect) to the world of "existence" (people and things) through the realization of the world of illusion.

We see the same thing in this famous poem in the *Collection of Ancient and Modern Japanese Poetry*:

> Yo no naka wa yume ka utsutsu ka utsutsu tomo yume tomo shirazu arite nakereba.
> (Is this world a mere dream or real? Since we are here and not here, I know not whether it is a dream or not.)

While *mujōkan* indeed teaches us "to be here and not be here," the important thing is that it reaffirms an awareness of both reality and nonreality.

To put it simply, the aesthetic feeling of *yūgen*, or "if hidden, it is the flower," does not seek a vivid, clear view of reality; nor does it take a casual attitude toward nonreality. It might be called a state of beauty in the *awai* between reality and nonreality. Needless to say, it leads to the aesthetic feeling of *wabi-sabi* (subdued simplicity), which seeks infinitely rich beauty in austere simplicity and frugality, not in luxury and flamboyance.

Incidentally, *yasashi* has another important aspect in that it contains a degree of performance and artificiality, which has something to do with self-restraint. Similarly, according to the

Iwanami Classical Dictionary, the word *nasake* (sympathy, pity), which is a synonym for *yasashi*, literally means "to *appear* to consciously do," just as *kanashige* means "to *appear* to be sad." Therefore, *nasake* contains a seeming falsification.

However, *nasake* has not been dismissed as a lie or hypocrisy. Rather it has been considered one of the requirements of an ideal person. For example, the following appears in *The Tale of Genji*: *Onoko wa, sashimo obosanu koto o dani, nasake no tame ni wa yoku iitsuzuketamau bekamereba* (The man [Prince Genji] was such a person who, out of *nasake*, would keep speaking well of that which he did not actually think was so). This type of sentiment is highly appreciated in Japan. Obviously, this kind of ex tempore consideration for others may sometimes contain a lie.

Nevertheless, *nasake* remained an important ethical and cultural attribute. It might, and sometimes should, be criticized as being essentially false, but this is not always the case. Sincerity and honesty are not the only ethical ideals.

This way of *nasake* is directly the way of *yasashi*. The kanji 優 can be read as *yasashi*, but its original meaning was performer or actor. Thus *yasashi* contains an element of performance and artificiality, of "showing."

To employ Dazai's wording, *yasashi* means to be sensitive to the "loneliness, bleakness, or bitterness" of others by incorporating performance and artificiality. This is the origin of Dazai's concept of "buffoonery." Needless to say, the feeling of distance contained in the ethics of *yasashi* and *nasake* is based on Kuki's so-called relative dualism.

Kanashi

Next, I will take up *kanashi* (sadness, grief). The playwright Yamada Taichi (b. 1934) wrote:

> I think that Japanese should pay more attention to "the sadness of life." I feel they should know the transience and helplessness of being human….
>
> Don't we expect too much from this world, both from others and from ourselves?
> What human beings can accomplish is not much, and our collective wisdom does not amount to much. And how much less can an individual do! If we think we have accomplished something of significance, it will not be long before we realize the transience of what we have done.
>
> In this way mankind is a sad thing. If nothing else, I hope never to forget this.
>
> (*Ikiru kanashimi* [The Sadness of Life])

The writer Itsuki Hiroyuki (b. 1932) said something similar when he remarked that what is required of modern Japan, which is now "as dry as a bone and lacking the weight of life," is *nasake* for others and the sentiment of *kanashi* (*Ima o ikiru chikara* [The Power to Live in the Present]).

According to the *Iwanami Classical Dictionary*, the basic meaning of *kanashi* is "a heart-rending feeling when confronting something that is far beyond one's power. It is probably a cognate of the verb *kane* (can't do)." In the meaning of deeply sensing our own finiteness and impotence when losing or being separated from an important person or thing, *kanashi* has been in common use as early as the *Man'yōshū*.

However, *kanashi* written 愛し and meaning "beloved" or "endearing" was not unusual, as seen in this excerpt from *The Tale of Ise*: *Hitotsu ko ni sae arikereba ito kanashū shita-maikeri* (As her only child, she was affectionate to him). In the *Man'yōshū*, *kanashi* appears in a poem by Ōtomo no Yakamochi indicating the solitude of living alone in the world of nature and the universe: *Uraura ni tereru haruhi ni hibari agari kokoro-kanashi mo hitori shi omoeba* (A lark flies up into the mild spring sky. All alone and lost in thought, I can't help feeling sad).

Considering the scope and depth of feeling expressed by the word *kanashi*, it is understandable that it should involve a number of important issues regarding the Japanese way of living and dying.

Nishida Kitarō declared, "Philosophy begins from the fact of our contradictory self-identity. The motive of philosophy must be the profound pathos of life, not intellectual 'surprise'" (*Basho no jiko-gentei to shite no ishiki sayō* [Mechanism of Consciousness as Locational Self-Restriction]). He further says:

> We live to die. We can say that death and grief lie at the bottom of every living thing.... To live is to die.... We ultimately end up seeing ourselves through grief.
> (*Ippansha no jikakuteki taikei* [The System of Universals in Self-Awareness])

In Nishida's thought, *kanashimi* (sorrow) is, simply put, a feeling about the self-contradiction of human existence that shapes the life of a mortal being. That is, we can call it a feeling in the *awai* between finiteness and infiniteness. *Mizukara* is mortal finiteness within the infiniteness of *onozukara*, but the finiteness cannot integrate and unify the infiniteness.

To put it more concretely, we human beings are within *onozukara* like bees, birds, or trees, but we are not completely incorporated and integrated into that function. There are *mizukara* feelings—this self, this self-consciousness—which are incorporated into *onozukara* but cannot be easily dissipated or disintegrated there. *Kanashimi* is evoked only in the *awai* between *onozukara* and *mizukara*.

And, importantly, it is assumed that we can make a connection with the *onozukara* (the gods, the Buddha) when we grieve (*kanashimu*) over our sorrow (*kanashimi*), as was the case with Nishida. The philosopher Tsunashima Ryōsen (1873–1907) wrote:

> Behold, the key to a nirvana that transcends grief has been secretly placed in grief itself since the eternal beginning of the world.
>
> Grief itself is halfway to salvation.... God first came to us in the form of grief. Within grief there is a kind of power that is not devoid of meaning. By experiencing grief and through grief, we can possess a certain something that transcends grief.... Grief itself is a kind of grace, the attainment of unification of God and Man.
>
> (*Shinkyōroku* [Record of Echoes from the Heart])

He suggests that if there is something like God or the Buddha, He will come to us first of all in the form of grief. That is why he says that grief itself is already an expression of a relationship between God and Man, which is halfway to salvation. Kaneko Daiei says much the same thing:

> I wonder why Japanese people do not grieve more. Today, what is truly lacking among the Japanese is grief, I think. Only in sorrow can we feel the spirit of the Buddha. We must be able to truly grieve. Grief should be the catalyst to feel mercy. Only in the depths of grief, I believe, will we be able to realize the mercy of the Buddha.
>
> ("Tariki hongan," *Watashi no jinseikan* ["Reliance on the Other," My View of Life])

By experiencing the *kanashimi* (sorrow) of human existence we eventually merge with the Great Compassion of the Buddha.

Kanashimi is a metaphysical emotion in the *awai* between *onozukara* (which encompasses things like God or Buddha) and *mizukara*, as well as being an ethical emotion toward neighboring others by realizing that metaphysical emotion. Motoori Norinaga states that we invariably put *kanashimi* into words when it becomes unbearable, and by expressing it and relating it to others and gaining their empathy, we come to feel deeply consoled and achieve a sense of relief.

There is also the word *yarikirenai*, which means that we cannot direct our unbearable feelings anywhere or make them understood by anyone. Norinaga explains that, in the process of living, people desperately need others or places to direct these feelings. He explains that being abundantly endowed with this type of sensibility and empathy is essential to human life.

Of course, *kanashimi* is basically a negative emotion, but as I discussed several times above, there are values, meanings, and *omoshiroshi* that do not emerge without the medium of *mizukara* finiteness or negativity. In this sense, *kanashimi* is not a mere emotion confined to our *mizukara*, but an important sentiment expressed in the *awai* with *onozukara* as well as in the *awai* connecting with neighboring others.

Sayōnara

Lastly, I will take up the salutation *sayōnara*.

Sayōnara, and its alternative *saraba*, are conjunctives, literally meaning "if it must be so." They convey the idea that if one accepts what has happened heretofore, one can expect certain occurrences hereafter. From this origin they have come to be employed as independent words of farewell. As with many other such expressions, they seem to have been used in this way since the Heian period.

It has been pointed out by Araki Hiroyuki (1924–99) in *Yamato kotoba no jinruigaku* (An Anthropology of Archaic Japanese) that there lies within the Japanese people the unique notion that before moving on to subsequent events, one must come to a standstill and confirm the present situation. That is, we can't proceed without such confirmation.

Then, what is exactly confirmed by *sayōnara*? Of course, since the word is essentially a salutation, we do not always make such confirmations consciously. However, looking at the word anew, I can point out two things.

One is that it is a confirmation of various events that have taken *mizukara* by a person prior to a parting. *Sayōnara* is a confirmation and summarization of past events and seems to imply an acceptance or connection of ourselves to future events.

In "*Shi no igaku*" *e no nikki* (Diary of "A Medical Study of Death") Yanagida Kunio says that modern times are a "period in which we create our own death." To "create our own death" means to summarize, complete, and conclude our own life in some form. It is as if by creating our own life story we can come to terms with our own death and accept it. It means to verbally summarize the content of "if it must be so," whereby we connect ourselves to the hereafter in our death and the world thereafter.

On the other hand, however, even though we connect the various events that we, as a self, have initiated thus far, it does not make a "story." We also have to confirm that there are events, including the four inevitabilities in human life (birth, aging, sickness, and death), that cannot be controlled by any person given life in this world. This is, in a sense, a confirmation of *onozukara*. This means to approve of and accept the inevitable movement of the more universal "if it must be so, it must be so."

The travel writer Anne Morrow Lindbergh wrote that she did not know of any word as beautiful as *sayōnara* for saying goodbye. She interpreted the word in this way:

> For Sayonara, literally translated, "Since it must be so,"
> of all the good-bys I have heard is the most beautiful....
>
> But Sayonara says neither too much nor too little. It is a simple acceptance of fact. All understanding of life lies in its limits. All emotion, smoldering, is banked up behind it. But it says nothing. It is really the unspoken good-by, the pressure of a hand, "Sayonara."
>
> *(North to the Orient)*

While Lindbergh understood that there are things in this world that are beyond our control, including encounters and partings, the Japanese quietly accept this as "if it must be so, it must be so" with a parting *sayōnara*.

Various life events happen in the *awai* between voluntary *mizukara* and involuntary *onozukara*, both being in conflict with one another. As I have said earlier, *sayōnara* implies "if it must be so, it must be so," even if it is not always consciously present in the mind.

There is one more important thing. I said earlier that *sayōnara* was originally a conjunctive, or a connecting word. I meant that it is confined to a confirmation of the past and that people part ways without knowing what the future will hold.

I believe the phrase contains the notion that, by confirming and summarizing the present based firmly on the past, and that without questioning what might happen in the future, we will be able to connect the two and get along in one form or another.

Concerning the parting brought about by death, we have the following:

But then, I'm alive at this moment, I'm alive today, and who knows whether tomorrow may bring a new light…. The world is fine as it is; everything is perfectly made. Isn't it best to live in that world like an ordinary person? This is the kind of thinking that I'm engrossed in. Not to have thoughts that one is special all by oneself but to live just like other ordinary fellows. I feel this may be what it takes to bring down the light of the true Heaven.

(Masamune Hakuchō, *Bungaku seikatsu no rokujūnen* [Sixty Years of a Literary Life])

That I will die is no different from adding tomorrow to today. (Myōe, *Gyōjōki* [Journal of General Behavior])

In these examples we can see the underlying notion that, by confirming and summarizing the past, we can somehow connect ourselves to what lies in the future.

Today *sayōnara* is used less frequently than heretofore, but its more colloquial versions——*sore dewa*, *dewa*, and *jā*—all have the same meaning. When we consciously say *jā* to one another in parting, even as an act of mourning, we are expressing the wisdom contained in the word *sayōnara*.

We can find the same nuanced meaning, I think, in "Flower petals fall, but the flower endures."

BIBLIOGRAPHY

Arai Man. *Jiyūyaku hannya shingyō* (The Heart Sutra: A Free Translation). Asahi Shimbun, 2005.

Arakawa Hiromu. *Hagane no renkinjutsushi* (Fullmetal Alchemist). Square Enix, 2010.

Araki Hiroyuki. *Yamato kotoba no jinruigaku* (An Anthropology of Archaic Japanese). Asahi Sensho, 1985.

———. *Nihongo ga mieru to eigo mo mieru* (You Can Understand English If You Can Understand Japanese). Chuko Shinsho, 1994.

Daijirin (Great Forest of Words). Sanseido, 1988.

Dazai Osamu. "Kawamori Yoshizō ate shokan" (Letters to Kawamori Yoshizō). In *Dazai Osamu zenshū 12* (The Complete Works of Dazai Osamu, vol. 12). Chikuma Shobo, 1999.

Fukuzawa Yukichi. *Fuku-ō hyakuwa* (One Hundred Discourses of Fukuzawa) and others. In *Fukuzawa Yukichi Chosakushū* (The Complete Works of Fukuzawa Yukichi). Keio University Press, 2002–2003.

Gikeiki (The Chronicle of Yoshitsune). In *Shinpen Nihon koten bungaku zenshū 62* (A New Edition of the Complete Anthology of Classical Japanese Literature, vol. 62). Shogakukan, 1999.

Hata Kōhei. *Migomori no umi* (A Lake to Hide In). In *Hata Kōhei umi no hon 16* (Lake Books by Hata Kōhei, vol.16). Umi no Hon Hanmoto, 1990.

Heike monogatari (The Tale of the Heike). In *Nihon koten bungaku taikei dai 32-33* (Compendium of Japanese Classic Literature, vol. 32-33). Iwanami Shoten, 1959-60.

Hokkukyō (Dhammapada). Kodansha, 1985.

"I am a thousand winds that blow." Translated into Japanese by Arai Man as *Sen no kaze ni natte* (Kodansha, 2003).

Inoue Yasushi. "Jinsei" (Human Life), *Kitaguni* (The Northern Land). In *Inoue Yasushi zenshū 1* (The Complete Works of Inoue Yasushi, vol. 1). Shinchosha, 1995.

Ishimure Michiko. "Umi wa mada hikari" (The Sea Still Shines). In *Shisō no kagaku dainanaji* (Science of Thought No. 7), *Minomata no ima* (Minomata Today). Shiso no Kagakusha, 1986.

Isobe Tadamasa. *"Mujō" no kōzō* (The Structure of *"Mujō"*). Kodansha, 1976.

Itsuki Hiroyuki. *Ima o ikiru chikara* (The Power to Live in the Present). Kadokawa, 2008.

Jankélévitch, Vladimir. *La mort*. Paris: Flammarion, 1966. Translated into Japanese by Nakazawa Norio as *Shi* (Misuzu Shobo, 1978).

Jiku no jidai I / Jiku no jidai II: Ikani mirai o kōsō shiuru ka (Axial Age I / Axial Age II: How Can We Design the Future?). Graduate School of Humanities and Social Sciences, University of Tokyo, 2009.

Kaibara Ekken. *Wazoku dōjikun* (A Guide to Japanese Customs for Children). In *Yōjōkun, Wazoku dōjikun* (Principles for Healthy Living and a Guide to Japanese Customs for Children). Iwanami Shoten, 1961.

Kamo no Chōmei. *Mumyōshō* (The Nameless Treatise). In *Karon-shū, nōgakuron-shū* (Collection of Treatises on Waka Poetry and Noh), *Nihon koten bungaku taikei dai 65* (Compendium of Japanese Classic Literature, vol. 65). Iwanami Shoten, 1961.

Kaneko Daiei. *Tannishō ryōge* (Understanding the *Tannishō*). In *Kaneko Daiei senshū dai 15 kan* (Selected Works of Kaneko Daiei, vol. 15). Zaike Bukkyo Kyokai, 1956. First published as *Iyaku, Tannishō* (Zenjinsha, 1949).

———. "Tariki hongan," *Watashi no jinseikan* ("Reliance on the Other," My View Of Life), "Jinsei no yukue," *Jūnishō* ("The Destination of Life," Twelfth Annotation) and others. In *Kaneko Daiei zuisōshū* (The Collected Essays of Kaneko Daiei). Kyoto:Yukonsha, 1972.

Kanjigen (The Origin of Chinese Characters). Gakushu Kenkyusha, 2001.

Karaki Junzō. *Mujō* (Impermanence). Chikuma Shobo, 1964.

———. *Shi to shi* (Poetry and Death). Bungeishunju, 1969.

Kimura Bin. *Aida* (In-Between Space). Kobundo, 1988.

———. *Gūzensei no seishin byōri* (The Psychopathology of Contingency). Iwanami Gendai Bunko, 2000.

Kiyozawa Manshi. *Tariki-mon tetsugaku gaikotsu shikō* (An Effort to Outline a Philosophy that Leads to the Other Power) and others. In *Kiyozawa Manshi zenshū* (The Complete Works of Kiyozawa Manshi). Iwanami Shoten, 2002.

Kojiki (A Record of Ancient Matters). In *Shinpen Nihon koten bungaku zenshū 1* (A New Edition of the Complete Anthology of Classical Japanese Literature, vol. 1). Shogakukan, 1997.

Kokin wakashū (Collection of Japanese Poems of Ancient and Modern

Times). In *Nihon koten bungaku taikei dai* 8 (Compendium of Japanese Classic Literature, vol. 8). Iwanami Shoten, 1958.

Kuki Shūzō. "Nihonteki seikaku" (The Japanese Character) and others. In *Kuki Shūzō zenshū* (The Complete Works of Kuki Shūzō). Iwanami Shoten, 1981.

Lindbergh, Anne Morrow. *North to the Orient*. New York: Harcourt Brace & Co., 1935. Translated into Japanese by Nakamura Taeko as *Tsubasa yo, kita ni* (Misuzu Shobo, 2002).

Maki Yūsuke. "Shikisokuzekū to kūsokuzeshiki: Tōtetsu no kiwami no tenkai" (Form Is Emptiness and Emptiness Is Form: Transformation of the Extreme Lucidity). In *Kiryū no naru oto* (The Sound of Airstreams). Chikuma Bunko, 1986.

Man'yōshū (Collection of Ten Thousand Leaves). In *Nihon koten bungaku taikei* dai 4-7 (Compendium of Japanese Classic Literature, vol. 4-7). Iwanami Shoten, 1957-62.

Maruyama Masao. *Rekishi ishiki no "kosō"* (The "Ancient Layer" of Historical Consciousness). In *Rekishi shisōshū* (Anthology of the Philosophy of History), *Nihon no shisō dai 6* (Japanese Thought, vol. 6). Chikuma Shobo, 1972.

Masamune Hakuchō. *Bungaku seikatsu no rokujūnen* (Sixty Years of a Literary Life). In *Masamune Hakuchō zenshū dai 13 kan* (The Complete Works of Masamune Hakuchō, vol. 13). Shinchosha, 1983.

Masuda Shōzō. *Nō no hyogen* (Expressions of Noh). Chuko Shinsho, 1971.

Matsubara Taidō. *Hannya shingyō nyūmon* (Introduction to the Heart Sutra). In *Matsubara Taidō zenshū 1* (The Complete Works of Matsubara Taidō, vol. 1). Shodensha, 1990.

Miki Kiyoshi. *Tetsugaku nyūmon* (An Introduction to Philosophy) and others. In *Miki Kiyoshi zenshū* (The Complete Works of Miki Kiyoshi). Iwanami Shoten, 1966.

Mita Munesuke. *Gendai Nihon no kankaku to shisō* (Thought and Sensibility in Modern Japan). Kodansha, 1995.

Miyazawa Kenji. "Aomori banka" (Aomori Lament) and others. In *Miyazawa Kenji zenshū* (The Complete Works of Miyazawa Kenji). Chikuma Bunko, 1986.

Motoori Norinaga. *Naobi no mitama* (The Way of the Gods), *Suzunoya tōmonroku* (Dialogue at Suzunoya), and others. In *Motoori Norinaga zenshū* (The Complete Works of Motoori Norinaga). Chikuma Shobo, 1968.

Murakami Haruki. *1973 nen no pinbōru* (Pinball, 1973). Kodansha Bunko, 1983.

Myōe. *Gyōjōki* (Journal of General Behavior). In *Myōe shōnin-shū* (Collected Writings of the Venerable Myōe). Iwanami Bunko, 1981.

Nakae Chōmin. *Zoku ichinen yūhan* (Sequel to a Year and a Half). In *Meiji bungaku zenshū 13* (The Complete Works of Meiji Literature, vol. 13). Chikuma Shobo, 1967.

Nakahara Chūya. "Tsukiyo no hamabe" (The Beach on a Moonlit Night). In *Nakahara Chūya shishū* (The Collected Poetry of Nakahara Chūya). Shincho Bunko, 2000.

Natsume Sōseki. *Sorekara* (And Then). Shincho Bunko, 1992.

Ninomiya Sontoku. *Ninomiya yawa* (Night Chats with Old Man Ninomiya) and others. In *Ninomiya Sontoku zenshū* (The Complete Works of Ninomiya Sontoku). Ryukei Shosha, 1977.

Nishida Kitarō. "*Kokubungakushi kōwa*" no jo (Introduction to "The History of Japanese Literature") and others. In *Shisaku to taiken* (Speculation and Experience). Iwanami Bunko, 1980.

Onō Susumu. *Nihongo no nenrin* (Growth Rings of the Japanese Language). Shincho Bunko, 1966.

——— et al., eds. *Iwanami kogo jiten* (Iwanami Classical Japanese Dictionary). Iwanami Shoten, 1974.

Sagara Tōru. *Ichigū ni tatsu* (Stand in a Corner) and others. In *Sagara Tōru chosakushū* (The Collected Writings of Sagara Tōru). Perikansha, 1992.

Saichō. *Ganmon* (A Prayer). In *Saichō–Kūkai-shū* (The Collected Works of Saichō and Kūkai), *Nihon no shisō dai 1* (Japanese Thought, vol.1). Chikuma Shobo, 1969.

Saint-Exupéry, Antoine de. *The Little Prince*. New York: Reynal and Hitchcock, 1943. Translated into Japanese by Naito Arō as *Hoshi no ōji-sama* (Iwanami Shoten, 2000).

Sakaguchi Ango. *Bungaku no furusato* (The Ancestral Home of Literature). In *Sakaguchi Ango zenshū 14* (The Complete Works of Sakaguchi Ango, vol. 14). Chikuma Bunko, 1990.

Shiga Naoya. *An'ya kōro* (A Dark Night's Passing) and others. In *Shiga Naoya zenshū* (The Complete Works of Shiga Naoya). Iwanami Shoten, 1999.

Shinjigen (New Font of Words). Kadokawa Shoten, 1968.

Shin kokin wakashū (New Collection of Ancient and Modern Japanese Poetry). In *Nihon koten bungaku taikei dai 28* (Compendium of Japanese Classic Literature, vol. 28). Iwanami Shoten, 1958.

Shinkei. *Shinkei hōin teikin* (Priest Shinkei's Domestic Lessons). In *Chūsei no bungaku, renka ronshū* 3 (Collection of Medieval Literature and Linked Poetry 3). Miyai Shoten, 1985.

Shinran. *Mattōshō* (Last Letters of Shinran). In *Shinranshū* (The Collected Works of Shinran), *Nihon no shisō dai* 3 (Japanese Thought, vol. 3). Chikuma Shobo, 1968.

Shitahodo Yūkichi. *Tendō to jindō: Ninomiya Sontoku no tetsugaku* (Heaven's Way and Man's Way: The Philosophy of Ninomiya Sontoku). Iwanami Shoten, 1942.

Shogakukan Nihon kokugo daijiten (Shogakukan Complete Japanese Language Dictionary). Shogakukan, 2000.

Sudō Matsuo. *Shiga Naoya no shizen* (Nature in Shiga Naoya). Meiji Shoin, 1979.

Takeuchi Seiichi. *Jikochōetsu no shisō: Kindai Nihon no nihirizumu* (The Philosophy of Self-Transcendence: Nihilism in Modern Japan). Perikansha, 1988.

―――. *Nihonjin wa "yasashii" no ka: Nihon seishinshi nyūmon* (Are Japanese *Yasashii*?: Introduction to the Spiritual History of Japan). Chikuma Shinsho, 1994.

―――. *"Onozukara" to "mizukara": Nihon shisō no kisō* ("*Onozukara*" and "*Mizukara*": The Substratum of Japanese Thought). Shunjusha, 2004.

―――. *"Hakanasa" to Nihonjin: Mujō no Nihon seishinshi* (*Hakanasa* and the Japanese People: Transience in the Spiritual History of Japan). Heibonsha Shinsho, 2007.

―――. *Nihonjin wa naze "sayōnara" to wakareru no ka* (Why Japanese Say "Sayonara" on Parting). Chikuma Shinsho, 2009.

―――. *"Kanashimi" no tetsugaku: Nihon seishinshi no minamoto o saguru* (The Philosophy of "Sorrow": Seeking the Fountainhead of Japanese Spiritual History). NHK Books, 2009.

―――. *Yamato kotoba de tetsugaku suru: "Onozukara" to "mizukara" no awai de* (Philosophizing in Archaic Japanese: The Boundary between "*Onozukara*" and "*Mizukara*"). Shunjusha, 2012.

――― and Kim Tae-Chang, eds. *"Onozukara" to "mizukara" no awai: Kōkyō suru sekai o Nihon shisō ni saguru* (The Boundary between "*Onozukara*" and "*Mizukara*": In Search of a Public Philosophy in Japanese Thought). University of Tokyo Press, 2010.

Tannishō (Lamentations of Divergences). Iwanami Bunko, 1981.

Tayama Katai. *Futon* (The Quilt) and others. In *Katai zenshū* (The Complete Works of Katai). Bunsendo Shoten, 1974.

Tendō Arata. *Itamu hito* (The Mourner). Bungeishunju, 2008.

Tokyo Shoseki. *Rinri* (Ethics). Tokyo Shoseki, 2002.

Tsunashima Ryōsen. *Shinkyōroku* (Record of Echoes from the Heart). In *Ryōsen zenshū* dai 5 kan (The Complete Works of Ryōsen, vol. 5). Shunjusha, 1921.

Uchimura Kanzō. *Yo wa ikanishite kirisuto shinto to narishika* (How I Became a Christian). Kadokawa Bunko, 1955.

Washida Kiyokazu. *Oi no kūhaku* (The Vacuity of Old Age). Kobundo, 2003.

Yamada Taichi, ed. *Ikiru kanashimi* (The Sadness of Life). Chikuma Shobo, 1991.

Yamazaki Masakazu. *Konton kara no hyōgen* (Expression Out of Chaos). Kyoto: PHP Institute, 1977.

Yanagita Kunio. *Senzo no hanashi* (About Our Ancestors). Chikuma Shobo, 1946.

Yanagida Kunio. *"Shi no igaku" e no nikki* (Diary for "A Medical Study of Death"). Shincho Bunko, 1999.

———. *Kotoba no chikara, ikiru chikara* (The Power of Words, the Power to Live). Shincho Bunko, 2005.

———. *"Jinsei no kotae" no dashikata* (How to Discover "the Answer to Human Life"). Shinchosha, 2004.

Yoshida Kenkō. *Tsurezuregusa* (Essays in Idleness). In *Shinpen Nihon koten bungaku zenshū 44* (A New Edition of the Complete Anthology of Classical Japanese Literature, vol. 44). Shogakukan, 1994.

Zeami Motokiyo. *Fūshikaden* (Transmission of the Flower through the Forms), *Kintōsho* (Book of the Golden Island), and others. In *Zeami, Zenchiku* (Zeami and Zenchiku). Iwanami Shoten, 1974.

———. *Obasute* (The Discarded Crone) and others. In *Yōkyoku hyakuban* (The One Hundred Chanting Books of Noh), *Shin Nihon koten bungaku taikei 57* (Compendium of Japanese Classic Literature, vol. 57). Iwanami Shoten, 1998.

Zōagonkyō (Samyukta Agama). In *Shinkokuyaku daizōkyō* (A New Japanese Translation of the Daizōkyō). Daizo Shuppan, 2004.

*All Japanese books published in Tokyo unless otherwise noted.
Macrons have been omitted from the name of publishers.

INDEX

A
About Our Ancestors, 9
Absolute Other, 24, 25
Account of My Hut, An, 125
aida, 133, 164; defined, 162
Aida. See *In-Between Space*
akirame: resignation and clarification, 123
Akutagawa Ryūnosuke, 150, 151
Amaterasu Ōmikami, 105, 115; *omoshiroshi*, 107, 108
Amida, 17, 24, 84, 93, 94, 121, 161, 165; *jinen*, 149; Shinran, 120
An'ya kōro. See *Dark Night's Passing, A*
Analects of Master Ninomiya, 156
Ancestral Home of Literature, The, 152
And Then, 20
Anne Morrow Lindbergh, 180, 181
anthropocentrism, 39, 40, 47
Anthropology of Archaic Japanese, An, 179
"Aomori banka." See "Aomori Lament"
"Aomori Lament," 75
Arai Man, 55, 58, 63, 80
Arakawa Hiromu, 137, 140
Araki Hiroyuki, 21, 22, 179
arigatai, 54, 57, 58, 62, 129; *Essays in Idleness*, 60
arigatashi, 128. See also *arigatai*
At Kinosaki, 52
Avatamsaka Sutra, 57
awai, 26, 31, 47, 50, 94, 127, 141, 161; *aida*, 133; as philosophical issue, 132-134; defined, 162, 163; ethics, 162, 166, 169; *Fullmetal Alchemist*, 137, 139; happiness, 96, 97; *jōju* and *rakkyo*, 125; *kanashimi*, 179; Kuki Shūzō, 167, 169; loss of, 159; monism, 128; Ninomiya Sontoku, 154-158; Noh, 110; *shiawase*, 99, 129; Shinran, 150; theoretical framework, 132; "turns out," 164; Westernization, 158, 159; *yūgen*, 172, 173
aware, 62, 109; Zeami, 124

Axial Age I / Axial Age II: How Can We Design the Future? 135, 136

B
Banbutsu hatsugenshū. See *Remarks on All Things*
banbutsu no rei, 12
banji nyoi, 99, 100
Basho no jiko-gentei to shite no ishiki sayō. See *Mechanism of Consciousness as Locational Self-Restriction*
"Beach on a Moonlit Night, The," 64
"Becoming a Thousand Winds," 80
Book of the Golden Island, 110
brain death, 40, 138
Bungaku no furusato. See *Ancestral Home of Literature, The*
Bungaku seikatsu no rokujūnen. See *Sixty Years of a Literary Life*
Bungeiron. See *On the Literary Arts*
busy; kanji, 7

C
Christianity, 39, 47, 136; *tōtosa*, 41
Chronicle of Yoshitsune, The, 148
Collection of Old Tales, 97
Collection of Ten Thousand Leaves. See *Man'yōshū*
Commentaries on a Collection of Chinese Poetry That Includes Three Classic Styles. See *Santaishishō*
Commentaries on the Book of Great Wisdom, 97
contingency; Kuki Shūzō, 167; *New Collection of Ancient and Modern Japanese Poetry*, 145; *onozukara*, 103, 117, 146, 148; *shizen*, 147

D
Daikeishoshō. See *Commentaries on the Book of Great Wisdom*
Dark Night's Passing, A, 14

Dazai Osamu, 4, 169; gentleness, 170, 171; *yasashi*, 174
death of God, 27
death of man, 27-29
dekiru, 21
"Destination of Life, The," *Twelfth Annotation*, 90
"Dew on Shallot Leaves," 78, 79, 91
Dhammapada, 57, 62
Dialogue at Suzunoya, 119-121
Diary of "A Medical Study of Death," 180
Diary of Lady Murasaki, The, 163
Discarded Crone, The. See *Obasute*
Dōgen, 18
"Drop in the Nile, A," 18, 50-55
dualism, 158, 174; Kuki Shūzō, 167

E

Effort to Outline a Philosophy that Leads to the Other Power, An, 25
Eguchi, 108, 124
"eight million gods." See *yaoyorozu no kamigami*
emptiness is form. See *kūsokuzeshiki*
Encouragement of Learning, 49
end of the world, 3, 6, 30
end-of-life care, 138
environmental destruction, 27, 28
ephemeralness, 30, 63
Essays in Idleness, 48, 60
ethics, 96, 138, 169, 173, 174; *awai*, 137, 162, 166
Ethics (textbook), 38, 39
Expression Out of Chaos, 122
Expressions of Noh, 33

F

fate, 54, 58, 83, 165; contingency, 167, 168
flower, 29, 32, 34, 35, 67, 68, 71, 72, 75, 84, 88, 92, 173; as the dead, 87; eternal light, 86; Noh, 107, 108
flower petals fall, but the flower endures, 67, 71, 72, 85, 86, 87, 92, 182; Kaneko Daiei, 89; *Obasute*, 34
"Form Is Emptiness and Emptiness Is Form: Transformation of the Extreme Lucidity," 30, 31, 64
form is emptiness; emptiness is form. See *shikisokuzekū kūsokuzeshiki*
Fujimura Misao, 4
Fujioka Sakutarō, 69
Fuku-ō hyakuwa. See *One Hundred Discourses of Fukuzawa*
Fukuzawa Yukichi, 10-12; *Encouragement of Learning*, 49; *mu*, 15; mysteriousness, 41; *onozukara*, 13, 14
Fullmetal Alchemist, 137-140
"Funkawan (Nokutān)." See "Volcano Bay (Nocturne)"
furusato, 150, 152, 153
Fūshikaden. See *Transmission of the Flower through the Forms*
Futon. See *Quilt, The*

G

Gakumon no susume. See *Encouragement of Learning*
Ganmon, 57
Gathering Gems and Gaining Flowers. See *rakkyo*
Gendai Nihon no kankaku to shisō. See *Thought and Sensibility in Modern Japan*
gensō-ekō, 88, 89, 91
Gikeiki. See *Chronicle of Yoshitsune, The*
Ginga tetsudō no yoru. See *Night on the Galactic Railroad*
Godō sōan. See *Preliminary Thoughts on the Path to Enlightenment*
Golden Light Sutra, 143
gratitude, 54, 55, 58, 62, 101, 116, 128, 161, 164
Greek: logos, 39; philosophy, 136
grief. See *kanashi*
Growth Rings of the Japanese Language, 106

Guide to Japanese Customs for Children, A, 49
Gūzensei no mondai. See *Problem of Contingency, The*
Gūzensei no seishin byōri. See *Psychopathology of Contingency, The*
Gyōjōki. See *Journal of General Behavior*

H

Habu Yoshiharu, 10
Hachinoki. See *Potted Trees, The*
Hagane no renkinjutsushi. See *Fullmetal Alchemist*
hakanai, 6, 8, 9, 62, 63; meaning, 5; positive, 7
hakanasa, 2, 122
hakanashi, 8, 121, 123
hakaru, 5, 7, 28, 63; kanji, 6; *shiawase*, 99
hanikami, 169
Hannya shingyō nyūmon. See *Introduction to the Heart Sutra*
happiness, 78, 79, 81, 91-93, 99, 101-104, 112, 113, 116, 160, 161, 166. See also *shiawase*
Hata Kōhei, 59
Heart Sutra, 31, 66
Heart Sutra: A Free Translation, The, 55
Heaven's Way and Man's Way, 155
Heike monogatari. See *Tale of the Heike, The*
History of Japanese Literature, The, 69, 81, 83
Hōgen monogatari. See *Tale of Hōgen, The*
Hōjōki. See *Account of My Hut, An*
honrai muichibutsu, 11
How I Became a Christian, 19
How to Discover "the Answer to Human Life," 66, 67, 90
human dignity, 38, 39
Human Dignity as Found in Japanese Thought, 48
"Human Life," 58

I

"I," 18, 53, 58, 158-160. See also self
I novel, 22
ichigū, 18, 19, 34, 51, 117, 123; "Drop in the Nile, A," 52; *sumu*, 127
Ichigū-ness, 50, 52, 54
Ikiru kanashimi. See *Sadness of Life, The*
Ima o ikiru chikara. See *Power to Live in the Present, The*
Impermanence, 8
In-Between Space, 45
inochi, 42-44, 46, 56, 116, 117, 159
Inoue Nobutaka, 3
Inoue Yasushi, 58, 60
Inquiry into the Good, An, 70
Introduction to Philosophy, An, 20, 134
Introduction to the Heart Sutra, 34, 35
Ippansha no jikakuteki taikei. See *System of Universals in Self-Awareness, The*
Ise monogatari. See *Tale of Ise, The*
Ishimure Michiko, 28, 29, 85
Isobe Tadamasa, 122, 123, 134
Issues of Japanese Culture, 133
itami, 69-71; Miyazawa Kenji, 74; Nishida Kitarō, 82; versus *saiwai*, 81
itamu, 69-72, 75, 89; directionality, 88; *itoshisa*, 91; kanji, 69; *mizukara*, 94; Nishida Kitarō, 89; relationship with; *tamurau*, 86; Yanagida Kunio, 90
Itamu hito. See *Mourner, The*
Itsuki Hiroyuki, 175
iwau, 97, 102-104, 116
Izanagi, 114, 115, 117, 118
Izanami, 114, 115, 117, 118

J

"Japanese Character, The," 134
Jikochōetsu no shisō: Kindai Nihon no nihirizumu. See *Philosophy of Self-Transcendence: Nihilism in Modern Japan, The*
Jiku no jidai I / Jiku no jidai II—Ikani mirai o kōsō shiuru ka. See *Axial Age I /*

Axial Age II: How Can We Design the Future?
jinen, 24, 149
Jinmei no sonchō. See *Respect for Human Life*
"Jinsei." See "Human Life"
"Jinsei no kotae" no dashikata. See *How to Discover "the Answer to Human Life"*
"Jinsei no yukue," *Junishō.* See "Destination of Life, The," *Twelfth Annotation*
Jinseikan. See *Philosophy of Life, The*
Jiyūyaku hannya shingyō. See *Heart Sutra: A Free Translation, The*
jōju, 125, 127
Journal of General Behavior, 182

K
Kaibara Ekken, 49
"Kairosei." See "Dew on Shallot Leaves"
kakegae ga (no) nai, 53, 65
Kamo no Chōmei, 125, 172
kanashi, 119, 121, 169, 175; Itsuki Hiroyuki, 175; kanji, 176; Nishida Kitarō, 176; resignation, 123
kanashimi, 69, 74, 78, 177; Miyazawa Kenji, 79, 80
Kaneko Daiei, 34, 67, 85-87; grief, 178; life and death, 90; *tomurai* and *itamu*, 88, 89
Kant, 38
Karaki Junzō, 7-10, 12, 13, 27, 31, 134
karma, 161, 165
Kawamori Yoshizō ate shokan. See *Letters to Kawamori Yoshizō*
Kegonkyō, 57
Kimigayo, 115
Kimura Bin, 45, 47, 159
Kinosaki nite. See *At Kinosaki*
Kintōsho. See *Book of the Golden Island*
Kiryū no naru oto. See *Sound of Airstreams, The*
Kitaguni, 59
Kiyozawa Manshi, 25, 26, 34, 150, 165

Kohon setsuwashū. See *Collection of Old Tales*
"Koiwai Farm," 76
"Koiwai nōjō." See "Koiwai Farm"
Kojiki, 41, 113-115, 117, 118
Kokin wakashū. See *Collection of Ancient and Modern Japanese Poetry*
Kokubungakushi kōwa. See *History of Japanese Literature, The*
Konkōmyōsaishōōkyō. See *Golden Light Sutra*
Konton kara no hyōgen. See *Expression Out of Chaos*
Kotoba no chikara, ikiru chikara. See *Power of Words, the Power to Live, The*
Kuki Shūzō, 134, 167-169, 174
Kurokawa Sō, 2
kūsokuzeshiki, 34, 86

L
La mort, 68
Lake to Hide In, A, 59, 60
Lamentations of Divergences. See *Tannishō*
"Lament for the Transient World," 16, 121
Last Letters of Shinran, 121, 149
Letters to Kawamori Yoshizō, 169
life and death, 14, 15, 33, 52, 60, 86, 87, 117, 118, 120, 123, 140, 148, 180, 182
Little Prince, The, 80
Lotus Sutra, 75
love, 13, 43, 59, 60, 76, 81-85, 89, 93, 100, 139, 144, 145, 151, 168

M
ma, 144, 155
Magatsubi no Kami, 119
Maki Yūsuke, 30
Makura no sōshi. See *Pillow Book, The*
Man'yōshū, 16, 141, 170, 176
Maruyama Masao, 42, 114
Masamune Hakuchō, 182

Masuda Shōzō, 33, 34
Matsubara Taidō, 34, 86
Mattōshō. See *Last Letters of Shinran*
Meaning of Methods and Purposes, 66
Mechanism of Consciousness as Locational Self-Restriction, 176
medetai, 100-104, 110, 127, 129
medetashi, 97, 99, 100, 127-129
metaphysical desire, 168
metempsychosis, 139
Migomori no umi. See *Lake to Hide In, A*
Miki Kiyoshi, 20, 26, 134
Milky Way Railroad. See *Night on the Galactic Railroad*
Minamata, 29, 85
Mita Munesuke, 27, 32, 63, 64, 68, 135; death of man, 28; emptiness is form, 30; *onozukara*, 136; *shōgon*, 32; sublimation, 29, 84
Miyazawa Kenji, 74-81, 91, 93, 94, 96
mizukara, 19-25, 34, 35, 45, 47, 48, 50, 101, 107, 108, 112, 142, 149, 166, 168; absolute passivity, 46; and *awai*, 26, 31, 96, 97, 99, 150, 162, 177, 178; chance encounters, 164, 165; defined, 132, 133, 143; *Full Metal Alchemist*, 138, 140; humanism, 137; "I," 160-162; *ichigū*, 123; *iwau*, 103; kanji, 21, 134; *mujō-aware*, 121; Nishida Kitarō, 84; Ninomiya Sontoku, 156-158; Noh, 110, 124, 125; *omoshiroshi*, 179; once and only occurrence, 51; partial, 154; recognition, 17; Sakaguchi Ango, 150, 153, 173; *sayōnara*, 180, 181; *shiawase*, 98, 129; *shōgon*, 31; *sumu*, 127; *tamurau* and *itamu*, 94; *tezukara*, 146; Westernization, 158, 159
momentum of breath, 43, 46, 116, 117, 159
monotheism, 20
Motoori Norinaga, 17, 41, 80; *kanashimi*, 179; *mizukara*, 121; negative *onozukara*, 119; peace of mind, 120; *yarikirenai*, 179
Mourner, The, 71

mu, 13, 15, 16, 52
mugen, 23, 25, 26, 150
mujō, 2, 7, 8, 13, 16, 17, 31, 62, 129, 132, 133; Noh, 125; *onozukara*, 121; Yamazaki Masakazu, 122
Mujō. See *Impermanence*
"*Mujō*" *no kōzō*. See *Structure of "Mujō, The"*
mujōkan, 2, 5, 17, 121-124, 173. See also *mujō*
Mukonkyo no jidai. See *Time without Foundation, A*
Murakami Haruki, 5
Murasaki Shikibu nikki. See *Diary of Lady Murasaki, The*
"Musei dōkoku." See "Wailing Inaudibly"
musubi, 113-116
My View of Life, 89, 178
Myōe, 182

N

"Nairu no mizu no itteki." See "Drop in the Nile, A"
Nakae Chōmin, 12-15
Nakahara Chūya, 64
Nakazawa Norio, 68
Namu Amidabutsu, 86
Naobi no mitama. See *Way of the Gods, The*
Natsume Sōseki, 20
Naturalism, 24
Naturalist literature, 23, 24
nature. See *shizen*
Nature in Shiga Naoya, 54
nenbutsu, 73, 84, 86, 89, 92-94, 149, 161
New Collection of Ancient and Modern Japanese Poetry, 144, 146
Nichts, 13
Nietzsche, 4
Night Chats with Old Man Ninomiya, 49, 155, 157, 158
Night on the Galactic Railroad, 79, 92, 93

nihilism, 2, 4, 5, 7, 8, 13, 14, 30, 68, 122; Buddhism, 160; modern, 27, 28; origin, 159; Sakaguchi Ango, 153; Shinkei, 172

Nihon bunka no mondai. See *Issues of Japanese Culture*

Nihon shisō no naka no ningen no songen ni tsuite. See *Human Dignity as Found in Japanese Thought*

Nihongo ga mieru to eigo mo mieru. See *You Can Understand English If You Can Understand Japanese*

Nihongo no nenrin. See *Growth Rings of the Japanese Language*

"Nihonshi no ōin." See "Rhyme in Japanese Poetry"

"Nihonteki seikaku." See "Japanese Character, The"

Ninomiya-ō yawa. See *Night Chats with Old Man Ninomiya*

Ninomiya sensei goroku. See *Analects of Master Ninomiya*

Ninomiya Sontoku, 49; *awai*, 154, 158; *mizukara* and *onozukara*, 157; partialization, 156, 159

Nishida Kitarō, 26, 45, 69-71, 94, 176; *awai*, 133; *History of Japanese Literature, The*, 81-83, 176; *kanashimi*, 177; *mizukara*, 84; *tamurau* and *itamu*, 89

Nishie Masayuki, 165

Nō no hyōgen. See *Expressions of Noh*

Noh, 31-34, 71, 72, 104; *awai*, 110; *medetai* introduction, 110, 127; *mizukara*, 110; *omoshiroshi*, 104, 105, 107, 108; rhythm of life, 124; *sumu*, 125

North to the Orient, 181

Nurturing the Aged, 125, 128

O

Obasute, 32-34, 109, 124

"*Obasute*" *no kozetsu*. See *Isolation of "Obasute," The*

"Ohōtsuku banka." See "Okhotsk Lament"

Oi no kūhaku. See *Vacuity of Old Age, The*

"Okhotsk Lament," 77

omedetō, 100, 101

omoshiroi, 105, 110, 129. See also *omoshiroshi*

omoshiroshi, 104, 111, 127, 129, 166, 179; defined, 105, 106; *Eguchi*, 109; *mizukara*, 107; Noh, 105, 108; Zeami, 124

On the Literary Arts, 168, 169

One Hundred Discourses of Fukuzawa, 10, 13

Ōno Susumu, 106

onozukara, 13-17, 20, 22, 23, 25, 31, 34, 42, 48, 50, 52, 53, 96, 97, 99, 111, 123, 124, 127-129, 136-138, 140-149, 156, 157, 159-162, 164, 166, 173, 177-181; absolute other, 46; ambiguity, 144; Amida, 24; *awai*, 26; chance encounters, 165; contingency, 148; defined, 132, 133, 141; *iwau*, 103; Japanese gods, 41; kanji, 21, 134; *Kojiki*, 114; Motoori Norinaga, 120, 121; *mujō-aware*, 121; *New Collection of Ancient and Modern Japanese Poetry*, 144; omnipresent, 154; *omoshiro ya*, 110; otherness, 148; positive and negative functions, 117; prayer, 47; recognition, 13; relationship with *mizukara*, 45; rhythm of, 125; Sakaguchi Ango, 150, 153; Shinran, 121, 149; *shizen*, 132, 147, 158; *tamurai* and *itamu*, 94; two-edged, 118

onozukara no sugata. See *honpū no sugata*

organ transplant, 39, 40

Otogi zōshi, 98

Ōtomo no Yakamochi, 16, 121, 176

P

Pinball, 1973, 5

Philosophy of Life, The, 168

Philosophy of Self-Transcendence: Nihilism in Modern Japan, The, 158

Philosophy of "Sorrow," The, 74, 79-81

Pillow Book, The, 142

Poetry and Death, 134
Potted Trees, The, 147
Power of Words, the Power to Live, The, 65, 66
Power to Live in the Present, The, 175
Prajnaparamitahrdaya. *See* Heart Sutra
preciousness, 60, 64, 166, 168
Preliminary Thoughts on the Path to Enlightenment, 154
Priest Shinkei's Domestic Lessons, 172
Problem of Contingency, The, 167
Psychopathology of Contingency, The, 159
Pure Land, 32, 84, 88, 91-93, 160, 161

Q
Quilt, The, 23

R
rakkyo, 125, 127
Record of Ancient Matters, A. *See Kojiki*
Record of Echoes from the Heart, 177
"Reliance on the Other," *My View of Life*, 89, 178
religion, 3, 13, 30, 31, 149; Christianity, 39; Fukuzawa Yukichi, 14; Japanese belief, 46, 47; Japanese mythology, 19, 20; Nakae Chōmin, 14
Remarks on All Things, 155
Respect for Human Life, 42
Rinri. *See* Ethics.
"Rhyme in Japanese Poetry," 168

S
sachi, 97, 112, 113
sadness. *See kanashi*
Sadness of Life, The, 175
Sagara Tōru, 19, 32, 42, 47, 134; *tōtosa*, 116
Saichō, 18, 57
saiwai, 81, 97, 113; defined, 111; kanji, 112
Sakaguchi Ango, 33, 173; *furusato*, 153; *onozukara*, 150
Samyukta Agama, 57

Santaishishō, 97, 126
sarugaku, 104, 105
sayōnara, 179-182
"Sea Still Shines, The," 28
"Sekai o shōgon suru shisō." *See* "Thinking that Sublimates the World"
self: *awai*, 26, 99; *itai*, 160; kanji, 21, 134, 159, 160; *mizukara*, 19, 121, 132, 133, 143, 165, 177; *mujōkan*, 123; Ninomiya Sontoku, 156, 157; *onozukara*, 180; preciousness, 64; Sagara Tōru, 41, 42; Shiga Naoya, 17, 18; "the modern self," 53
self-recognition: "Drop in the Nile, A," 51, 52; *ichigū*-ness, 54
1973 nen no pinboru. *See Pinball, 1973*
"Sen no kaze ni natte." *See* "Becoming a Thousand Winds"
Senzo no hanashi. *See About Our Ancestors*
Sequel to a Year and a Half, 12
"Shi no igaku" e no nikki. *See Diary of "A Medical Study of Death"*
Shi to shi. *See Poetry and Death*
shiawase, 96, 103, 129, 166; *banji nyoi*, 99; defined, 97, 98; *iwau*, 10; two-edged *onozukara*, 118
Shiga Naoya, 14, 17, 18, 50, 52, 54, 55, 123; "Drop in the Nile, A," 53; *At Kinosaki*, 51; *mu*, 15
Shiga Naoya no shizen. *See Nature in Shiga Naoya*
shikisokuzekū kūsokuzeshiki, 30, 31, 34, 35, 55, 63, 64, 66-68, 162
"Shikisokuzekū to kūsokuzeshiki: Tōtetsu no kiwami no tenkai." *See* "Form Is Emptiness and Emptiness Is Form: Transformation of the Extreme Lucidity"
Shin kokin wakashū. *See New Collection of Ancient and Modern Japanese Poetry*
Shinkei, 172
Shinkei hōin teikin. *See Priest Shinkei's Domestic Lessons*

Shinkyōroku. See *Records of Echoes from the Heart*

Shinoda zuma, 139

Shinran, 17, 24-26, 89, 93, 94; *awai*, 150; *mizukara*, 121; mysteries of life, 120; *onozukara*, 121, 149; salvation, 94; self, 161

Shinto, 46, 47, 102

Shitahodo Yūkichi, 155

shizen, 54, 120, 132, 134, 148; defined, 147; *jinen*, 149; Kuki Shūzō, 169; nature, 158; *onozukara*, 147

shōgon, 29, 31, 32, 34; individual, 85; Noh, 34

Shoku Nihongi kayō. See *Songs and Poems from the Chronicles of Japan, Sequel*

Shūgyokutokka. See *Gathering Gems and Gaining Flowers*

Shushōgi. See *Meaning of Methods and Purposes*

Sixty Years of a Literary Life, 182

solitude, 34, 59, 60, 176; Sakaguchi Ango, 33, 153

Songs and Poems from the Chronicles of Japan, Sequel, 126

Sorekara. See *And Then*

sorrow. See *kanashimi*

soul, 14, 47, 48, 71, 72, 76, 80, 90, 138; of all things, 49; *tamashii*, 64, 66, 67

Sound of Airstreams, The, 30

Structure of "Mujō," The, 123

sublimation, 27-30-35, 68, 69; Ishimure Michiko, 85; Mita Munesuke, 84; Noh, 34

Sudō Matsuo, 54

sumu, 125-127

Suzunoya tōmonroku. See *Dialogue at Suzunoya*

System of Universals in Self-Awareness, The, 176

T

Taketori monogatari. See *Tale of the Bamboo Cutter*

Tale of Genji, The, 126, 142, 163, 174

Tale of Hōgen, The, 147

Tale of Ise, The, 112, 176

Tale of the Bamboo Cutter, 106

Tale of the Heike, The, 148, 171

tamashii, 64, 66, 67. See also soul

Tannishō, 25, 84, 92, 93, 160, 161

Tannishō ryōge. See *Understanding the Tannishō*

"Tariki hongan," *Watashi no jinseikan*. See "Reliance on the Other," *My View of Life*

Tariki-mon tetsugaku gaikotsu shikō. See *Effort to Outline a Philosophy that Leads to the Other Power, An*

Tayama Katai, 22

Tendō Arata, 71, 91

Tendō to jindō. See *Heaven's Way and Man's Way*

Tetsugaku nyūmon. See *Introduction to Philosophy, An*

"Thinking that Sublimates the World," 27, 29, 85

Thought and Sensibility in Modern Japan, 27

Time without Foundation, A, 3

tomurai, 74, 81, 85. See also *tomurau*

tomurau, 69, 72, 75; directionality, 88; general discussion, 69; *itoshisa*, 91; kanji, 71; *mizukara*, 94; Nishida Kitarō, 89; relationship with *itamu*, 86; Yanagida Kunio, 89

Tosa Diary, 141

Tosa nikki. See *Tosa Diary*

Tōtoi. See also *tōtosa*: *arigatai*, 58; *awai*, 166; *ichigū*, 51; meaning, 38; mysterious workings, 41; relationality, 65; Sagara Tōru, 42, 116; terminal care, 39, 40

tōtosa, 38, 40-42, 46, 50, 51, 54, 63, 116; *arigatai*, 58; Fukuzawa Yukichi, 12; *ichigū*, 51; Japanese view, 40; life and death, 52; Ninomiya Sontoku, 50; of man, 38; organ transplant, 40; relation-

ality, 64; Saigyō, 46; time, 58; unlimited, 42, 47
tōtoshi, 116
transience, 9, 12, 16, 17, 34, 54, 108, 109, 121, 122, 172, 175. See also *mujō*: Mita Munesuke, 64; preciousness of life, 168; *shikisokuzekū*, 86
Transmission of the Flower through the Forms, 104, 105, 107
"Tsukiyo no hamabe." See "Beach on a Moonlit Night, The"
Tsunashima Ryōsen, 177
Tsurezuregusa. See *Essays in Idleness*

U

Uchimura Kanzō, 19
"Umi wa mada hikari." See "Sea Still Shines, The"
Understanding the Tannishō, 86-88, 92
unusualness, 54, 58, 63, 64

V

Vacuity of Old Age, The, 6
Vast Nature, 15, 17
Vladimir Jankélévitch, 68
"Volcano Bay (Nocturne)," 77

W

"Wailing Inaudibly," 74, 79
wabi-sabi, 173
ware, 159, 160
Washida Kiyokazu, 6
watakushi shōsetsu. See I novel
watashi, 159; kanji, 160
Watashi no jinseikan. See *My View of Life*
Way of the Gods, The, 119
Wazoku dōjikun. See *Guide to Japanese Customs for Children, A*
"what is man," 138

Y

Yamada Taichi, 175
Yamato kotoba no jinruigaku. See *Anthropology of Archaic Japanese, An*
Yamazaki Masakazu, 122, 124
Yanagida Kunio, 66, 68, 81, 89; death, 180; Miyazawa Kenji, 80
Yanagita Kunio, 9, 10, 80
yaoyorozu no kamigami, 19, 42
yasashi: artificiality, 173; general discussion, 169; kanji, 170; meaning, 171; *nasake*, 174; transience, 172
yasashii. See *yasashi*
yin and yang, 154, 155
Yo wa ikanishite kirisuto shinto to narishika. See *How I Became a Christian*
"Yononaka no mujō o kanashiburu uta." See "Lament for the Transient World"
Yōrō. See *Nurturing the Aged*
Yoshida Kenkō, 48, 60, 61
You Can Understand English If You Can Understand Japanese, 21
yūgen, 25, 26, 150, 172, 173

Z

Zeami, 33, 104, 105, 115, 127; Eguchi, 109; exile, 110; flower, 107; Noh performance, 124, 125; *omoshiroshi*, 107; *sumu*, 126, 127; *yūgen*, 172
Zen no kenkyū. See *Inquiry into the Good, An*
Zoku ichinen yūhan. See *Sequel to a Year and a Half*

TAKEUCHI SEIICHI is professor emeritus at the University of Tokyo and the former chairperson of the Japanese Society for Ethics.

This book is based on the valedictory lecture given by the author at the Graduate School of Humanities and Social Sciences, Faculty of Letters of the University of Tokyo (January 2010). In addition, it is also composed of his lecture at the Gakushikai's dinner lecture event (May 2006), the "Multidisciplinary Exchange Exercise" lecture he gave at the University of Tokyo (January 2010), and his lecture at the Kamakura Women's University Research Institute (June 2010).

(英文版) 花びらは散る 花は散らない
——無常の日本思想
Flower Petals Fall, but the Flower Endures:
The Japanese Philosophy of Transience

2019年1月31日　第1刷発行

著 者
竹内 整一

翻訳・制作/発行所
一般財団法人出版文化産業振興財団
〒101-0051 東京都千代田区神田神保町3-12-3
電話　03-5211-7282(代)
ホームページ　http://www.jpic.or.jp/

印刷・製本所
株式会社ウイル・コーポレーション

定価はカバーに表示してあります。
本書の無断複写（コピー）、転載は著作権法の例外を除き、禁じられています。

Printed in Japan

©2011 Takeuchi Seiichi
ISBN 978-4-86658-069-2